'A wise, clear, warm and inclusive friend to help you through times of great sadness – whether your own or a loved one's. This book should be available on prescription.'
Sali Hughes, author of *Pretty Honest*

'When my life turned upside down, this is the book I wish I could have read. If anyone you know is in the depths of grief, [*How to Feel Better*] can show you how to be the friend they need.'
Decca Aitkenhead, author of *All at Sea*

'I devoured [*How to Feel Better*] in one sitting . . . a kind, honest and wise book about how to make a friend of sadness.'
Rachel Joyce, author of
The Unlikely Pilgrimage of Harold Fry

'The perfect choice for anyone keen . . . to make sense of any recent emotional upheaval'
Laura Barnett, author of *The Versions of Us*

'Wise, generous, a light, a balm, Cathy Rentzenbrink brightens the soul'
Megan Bradbury, author of *Everyone is Watching*

'Big-hearted . . . a shouldering survival guide for anyone whose own heart is breaking, or who knows someone else is hurting. There is healing balm here, but also much steeling, real-world wisdom'
The Bookseller

How to Feel Better

Cathy Rentzenbrink is the bestselling author of *The Last Act of Love, How to Feel Better, Dear Reader, Write It All Down* and *Everyone Is Still Alive*. She lives in Cornwall with her family.

How to Feel Better

to

Feel

Better

A guide to navigating the ebb and flow of life

Cathy Rentzenbrink

bluebird
books for life

First published 2017 by Picador

First published in paperback 2017 by Picador

This edition first published 2023 by Bluebird
an imprint of Pan Macmillan
The Smithson, 6 Briset Street, London EC1M 5NR
EU representative: Macmillan Publishers Ireland Ltd, 1st Floor,
The Liffey Trust Centre, 117–126 Sheriff Street Upper,
Dublin 1, D01 YC43
Associated companies throughout the world
www.panmacmillan.com

ISBN 978-1-0350-1425-5

1 3 5 7 9 8 6 4 2

A CIP catalogue record for this book is available from the British Library.

Printed and bound by CPI Group (UK) Ltd, Croydon, CR0 4YY

MIX
Paper | Supporting
responsible forestry
FSC® C116313
www.fsc.org

Visit **www.panmacmillan.com/bluebird** to read more about all our books
and to buy them. You will also find features, author interviews and
news of any author events, and you can sign up for e-newsletters
so that you're always first to hear about our new releases.

For Erwyn and Matt,
and for everyone who has told me their story

I want to be honest; I think it gets you further
and also makes you feel better about yourself.
Anne Frank, *The Diary of a Young Girl*

What do we live for, if it is not to make life
less difficult to each other?
George Eliot, *Middlemarch*

Dear reader,

Hello and welcome. I'm pleased to see you. And concerned for you, and a little curious about what has brought you to me. My sweetheart, I want to say I'm sorry. I wish you didn't need this book. I wish you already felt really good. But given that you don't, I'm glad you're here and that you found your way to me and I will be honoured if I can – even in a tiny way – help you get on the path to feeling better.

What do I mean by better? Do I mean everything is fixed and sorted and we are happy, energized and fulfilled all the time, and have all the answers to everything? I don't. I have not worked out how to achieve that for myself, but what I have learned to do when times are rough is focus instead on how to hold steady, how to feel just a little better, just a bit more able to get up and get on. When awful things happen, or when my mood crashes and everything is bleak, I have worked out what I need to do to keep the show on the road.

What qualifies me to offer advice on how to cope when the world behaves in a way we don't like? Well, I watched the person I loved most die a long, slow death. And I live with a bleak internal landscape that surprises anyone who only knows my fairly cheerful exterior. Mood swings. I'm up then I'm down. The micro-climate of me is highly variable. I like listening to the shipping forecast which often sounds as though it is describing what is happening inside my head; squally showers, thundery showers, sea state rough, becoming rougher later. Visibility poor, losing my identity, gale force ten. So those are my qualifications; experience of weathering internal and external turbulence. Pain is part of life and there is no point in pretending otherwise. But suffering is more optional. If life is a sea, then there are days when we get swirled around, and unceremoniously dunked. The trick is to roll with the waves, find our way back up to the surface, be a bobbing cork, not a sinking brick.

Life is hard and gritty and unfair and full of bumps and bad things happen to all people and we live in a consumer world where news outlets like us anxious because then we'll tune in more, and advertising promises us that happiness is just the right purchase away, so we think there is something wrong with us when we are miserable. All our human desires have been hacked and commoditized but we can wrest back control. We can run our own virus software. We can reconnect to what really matters.

None of this is easy. But if we want to stick around, if we commit to playing the game of life, there are things we can do to ease our path. We can bring in curiosity and amusement and a sense that we are learning new things and that we are a work in progress. We can understand that life is not a shop or a spa, and that we can't only order what we want from the menu. We can know that we only have one life, and ask what, at the end of it, we will wish we had done? Spent more time being angry and judgemental? Bought more stuff? I think there is a good chance we'll wish that we'd figured out how to spend more of our life in wonder, more of our time just looking at the world, up at the sky, or into the eyes of a baby, or playing with a kitten, or laughing with a friend.

One of my favourite things to do is teach writing workshops. Over the years I have learned that it really fuels my honesty and authenticity if I give everyone full permission to ignore my advice. 'All any writer can really do,' I say, as I stand at the front of the room looking at eager, curious, sometimes nervous faces, 'is say "this is what works for me". I will tell you what I know with an open and generous heart, trusting that you will decide what to do with that offering.' And that's what

I'm doing here. I've looked at the world and I'm telling you what works for me. This book could be called how *I* feel better but I give it to you with love and humility and a genuine desire to be in your service. I hope that what I have learned might be of use to you as you navigate on through the beautiful and occasionally stormy seas of life.

Introduction

Life hurts. Now, I'm not sure why we all find that so surprising but once upon a time I had a happy childhood and expected that things would get even better as I grew up. I was full of hope and an almost arrogant certainty that real life was waiting for me. I wanted to learn and live, and was hungry for experience.

Instead my heart was broken when my brother Matty was knocked over by a car on a dark road a mile from where we lived in Yorkshire. I was seventeen and he was sixteen. He was thirteen months younger than me and nine inches taller, full of jokes and laughter, a lovable, cheeky boy who shone in the classroom and on the football pitch. The customers of the pub our parents owned said he was too clever for his own good, but then they said that about me, too.

What happened next was complicated because he didn't die outright. Emergency brain surgery prevented his death; he was in a full coma for ten days and then his eyes slowly opened at the rate of a millimetre or so every few hours. Weeks turned into months turned into years, as we poured love, hope and work into his rehabilitation but he never made any further progress into consciousness. He lived on in a Persistent Vegetative State – ugly words for an ugly and terrible condition. It was another eight years and a complicated legal process before he finally, properly left this life, before we could have a funeral and try to mourn the loss of him.

After that I did what people often do when they're in pain: I created chaos for myself and others. As the years passed, I tried to get over my sorrow, to get on with life. Good things happened – I sobered up, learned to enjoy work, made friends and had a child –

but I always had this feeling of being stuck, that whether I wanted to or not, I just couldn't get past what had happened. My heart would always ache.

I wrote a book about it all called *The Last Act of Love*, and that helped. I felt a sense of pride that I had managed to wrestle this complex story on to the page and I loved that my brother's friends thought I had captured his strength, warmth and wit.

Perhaps the thing I was most grateful for was the way people came to talk to me at events or wrote me letters about the griefs and losses in their own lives. It was by listening to others that everything became clearer for me and I began to feel part of a community of damaged people, which sounds gloomy but was immensely reassuring. I realized how many of us look as though we're navigating life in an apparently success-ful or even happy way, yet are weighed down by burdens and exhausted from the effort of hiding our sadness.

Lots of people thanked me for showing them they weren't alone in their feelings and I came to see how much we all have in common, that all loss – from the untimely death of a loved one, through to the loss of innocence, all the way to having a bag stolen – feels as though it is specific to us, but is actually universal. I began to see that in sharing our suffering and acknowledging the pain of being human, we not only ease the burden on ourselves, but also help those around us to see themselves as part of the same whole.

After the book was published, people often asked me for advice about what to say to someone when the worst has happened, or what might help them. They asked me whether they could give *The Last Act of Love* to someone who had suffered a terrible loss. They worried, as I did, about imposing a sad and difficult story on someone already struggling under the weight of their own experience.

At around the same time, I came across the notion of 'content and process', a term used by therapists. Content is the thing that has happened, process is the attempt to work out how to accommodate it. I thought about how content is the thing specific to us – our own story – but process is what we have in common. We are all just blundering through, trying to work out how to live in a world that doesn't behave the way we want it to.

Could there be a way of sharing my process, of writing something with the specific purpose of consoling someone? Perhaps heartbreak is what happens on impact, and heartache is what we are left with as time passes, once the dust settles, when we are able to look up and around us but are still shrouded in sadness. What would have been useful for me to know as I navigated these states? If my first book was content, then perhaps my second would be process. I could spare the reader the agonies of the sad story but hope that lessons from along the way might be useful to someone, no matter what their own situation might be.

This is the book I wish I'd had when the worst happened, full of the advice I wish I'd been given. It's also the book I'd like to have beside me for whatever the future may hold. I wanted to pull all my thoughts together in one place, to have something to refer to when life took another twist, or started to look bleak around the edges.

I'm not a doctor, a therapist, a philosopher, a priest or an expert on anything. I'm just a human being who has thought a lot about how to be alive in this world. I don't want this to be difficult or sad. I poured the details of my anguish into my first book, but this is one that I hope you could safely give to someone without worrying about pushing them further into the abyss.

There were times in my past when I didn't want to be alive. I thought my heart couldn't bear the pain of the world and might one day just refuse to beat. I don't feel like that now. My heart still aches and I still pass through times of depression but I have learned how to manage it. I now know what to tell myself so that I can hold on. Even at my very worst, I still want to be alive, I just want to feel better. And there are lots of times when I experience joy beyond anything I thought possible.

I'm sharing my way through. I think of this book as a loving message in a bottle – tossed into the sea to wash up at the feet of someone in need. Take from it what you will.

I hope that nothing I say is in any way irresponsible or unhelpful and would encourage you to seek help from your GP, talk to someone you trust or call the Samaritans on 116 123 if you are distressed, depressed or otherwise concerned for your mental health.

Please, if it doesn't resonate with you then just put it down and read something else. I expect it to be chucked across the room a few times. 'A book?' I can hear you say, in your anger and grief. 'What use could a book possibly be when my heart has been ripped out?'

I've thrown a few books across the room in my time. I've hated people who have tried to offer me hope and I sullenly turned my nose up at lots of the advice I now offer here because I wasn't ready for it. But, despite the throwing, I have always trusted and relied on books and found them a source of both wisdom and comfort.

This is my far from perfect guide on how to be alive in this cruel but beautiful world. Something that always consoles me, that never fails to throw a chink of light into a dark day, is remembering that others have walked this path before me. I wrote this for myself, but also for you, so that even as your heart breaks and aches, and you can't imagine how you will ever feel better, you can know you are not alone.

What's Your Story?

Everyone has a backstory. From the moment of our birth, we are accumulating experiences and those experiences will be many shades of light and dark as we learn the meaning of both joy and pain. Lots of us have a defining thing – sometimes a death or a loss, but not necessarily – that is a source of grief, and often of guilt and shame. I didn't always know this. I used to think a talent for appearing fine and showing a false front to the world was specific to me. I'm glad I know now that I am far from alone in hiding my heartache from other people and pretending to feel better than I do.

Here are just a few stories that have been told to me by friends, or by people who have come to speak to me at events or who have got in touch with me after reading my book. What these people have in common is that they all appear to be on top of things. You would look at them and envy the apparent ease with which they stroll through life.

M was abused when she was a child. In every relationship she has ever had, she has worried about what point to share her difficult story. Once, she confided in a boyfriend and that was the last time she saw him. He just couldn't cope.

G's baby boy died inside her and she had to go ahead and give birth to his body. She was never able to conceive again. She tells no one about this but regularly has to field questions about why she doesn't have children. Often people speculate aloud that she cared more about her career than having kids.

F had a sister who died. Her parents made a shrine out of their house. As F grew older she escaped to university and never admitted to being anything other than an only child. She never took friends home. Years later, about to introduce her fiancé to her parents, she knew she'd have to tell him but couldn't bring herself to say the words so she wrote it down on a piece of paper and gave it to him on the train on the way there.

P's brother was knocked down and killed in front of him when he was twelve. As the oldest, he still feels somehow to blame.

At a book event, a smartly dressed man in late middle age lowered his voice to tell me that he had never forgotten being sent away to school when he was seven. There was such pain in the childlike eyes that looked out at me from his grown-up face.

One of my favourite conversations was with a beautiful woman who asked me if she was allowed to use the lessons in my book to get over splitting up with her boyfriend. 'I know it doesn't compare to other people's problems. I know it shouldn't matter to me so much, but it does,' she said. 'I thought I was going to have his children. I thought I knew what my life was going to be like and now I don't.' She helped me see how the way we try to impose a hierarchy on pain is really unhelpful for people who are suffering, making them feel they are less worthy of society's sympathy.

The truth is, it's not just about the big, dramatic stories. So many lives are full of difficulty. Having children can be fraught with pitfalls: there's the disaster of an unwanted pregnancy, the heartbreak of being unable to conceive, the realization that life with the cherished, longed-for child is so much harder than you could have imagined. Perhaps you have a baby who won't stop crying, a stubborn toddler or a teenager who appears to hate you.

I've often thought we underestimate the effects of work, of unexpected redundancy, say, or the impact of feeling bullied. Often people live with pain and illness, or simply – though, of course, it's far from simple – the feeling that they are not living life as it should be lived, that something is missing or has gone awry.

We have a tendency, us humans, to do almost anything in pursuit of distracting ourselves from our pain, so chaos and destruction often follow in the wake of the first wound. Lots of people have a toxic story that weaves itself around them like a particularly virulent species of poison ivy and is hard to hack off.

Sometimes I think I've done it. I have a new bit of therapy or a new insight and I feel free. But then I discover more tendrils have taken root in bits of me I didn't even know existed. At some point, often kicking and screaming, we have to accept that our experiences are part of who we are, whether we like it or not.

What I have learned is that almost everyone is struggling – whether they know it or not – with how to cope with their backstory. I do some prison visiting and find it humbling to be with people who are laden with big burdens. The saddest stories are found here: people who were not loved as children, for whom neglect was better than attention, who grew up with more pain than kindness, with no love, not even of the tough, undemonstrative variety.

Recently I discussed the idea of backstory with a prison reading group. They were of mixed ability, as is often the case in prison, because if you are struggling to survive as a kid, if your home is not a safe place, then education almost always takes a back seat. For all of the men I met, the library was a refuge and a comfort, a place where there is as much peace as it is possible to find inside.

I told them about Maya Angelou, how she said that there is no greater agony than carrying around an untold story. I explained backstory, asking everyone to imagine a new character arriving in a soap opera. What do we know about them at the start? How will we find out more? We had a bit of a laugh about the fact that on telly there is always significant signalling, those exaggerated stares that people pull to make it clear someone will turn out to be a baddie.

Everyone got it and I could see they were full of thoughts of their own backstories. One man said, 'Yeah, you've gotta be able to tell your own story. Else everything turns to chaos.'

And there, in that little room, it felt like the truest

thing I'd ever heard. How can we explain our lives and our actions to others when we can't acknowledge them ourselves?

It's the most important thing about us, surely? What has caused us pain, and how we have learned to carry on and – maybe, one day – find joy. That's what we should be talking to each other about on blind dates, not whether or not we have a good sense of humour or enjoy reading the Sunday papers, but what has hurt our hearts. For us to truly know one another we must be able to share our heartache.

This is hard to do. It's exposing, and we are frightened of revealing too much about ourselves. We all feel a desire to be understood that runs alongside a fear that no one will care. We worry that if people knew what we were really like, they'd run away.

Often I want to disassociate myself from my backstory. It doesn't seem fair or real. I'm too jolly, too happy, too funny to have been cast into such a sad story. 'No,' I want to say, 'there's been some mistake.

I'm supposed to be over there having carefree times and telling jokes. I'm not supposed to be here.'

So I pretend to be different. I put on a mask, as we all do, and make myself more likeable, less dangerous. We are so scared of appearing ugly or undesirable in front of people that we hide our scars under bright colours and fake smiles.

The other problem is that our stories might not make sense. Logic is not always our friend in working out why we are distressed, and, often, we are angry with ourselves for caring about something, or think that we should be over it by now. I think of my story as an octopus. All those tentacles, wriggling around, some fatter than others, some newer than others . . . (It's not an anatomically correct octopus, obviously.)

How can we tame it? Because the danger of an untold story is that it festers within, causing all sorts of problems. How can we liberate ourselves from it? We could talk to a friend, or a professional like a therapist, a counsellor or a religious person. I have found there is a powerful release in exhuming a long-held secret and saying it out loud to a fellow human, but if talking to someone feels too much, you could try writing it down. The page is there, empty and welcoming.

I didn't start writing my first book thinking that anyone would read it. Initially, the words were purely for myself, an attempt to take all of the pain and heartache from inside me and put it on to the page. It was far from easy and sometimes I felt as if I was bleeding all over my keyboard, but I'd think of what the customers in the pub I grew up in used to say when someone was sick after drinking too much: 'It's better off out than in.' I thought of it as a box of despair; it was big, unwieldy and difficult to get a grip on. As I unpacked the contents they became more manageable, lighter and easier to carry. More like a rucksack. And in daring to look again on the most painful scenes from my life, I also reconnected with the warmer, sweeter memories that had been trapped in the no-go area.

A kind therapist I saw said, 'We can't change the event, but we can look at your relationship with the event.' This is a good way to think about the things that have happened to us. We can't change the fact that they happened, but how we choose to think and speak about them in the future is up to us, and so is what we decide to do with the knowledge that we have unwillingly gained.

None of this is easy. I was out walking with my mother recently in the village where my parents live in Cornwall. London is flat and despite making resolutions to walk up escalators, I never do, so I always arrive in Cornwall out of shape. There's a circular walk we do that takes about an hour and includes a fiercely steep hill. On the first day I have to drag myself up it, but by the last day I skip up like a gazelle. We like to talk, my mother and I – we are always chatting – but it takes a few days before I can manage a conversation at the same time as walking up Ghost Hill. This always leads me to think that the harder and steeper the climb, the more difficult it is to find the breath, let alone the words.

Perhaps because I read too many novels, I often have this shadowy sense of parallel lives stretching out next to mine. My brother was not knocked over; he is in my life, we are close. Not only is he alive, but I am different: more joyful, more open, less frightened. I stand up straight, I don't ache because I'm not continually bracing my body against the pain of what might happen next. I could drive myself mad with this imagining, endlessly obsessing about a different, better world, inhabited by a different, stronger me. But I have learned that, impossible though it may seem, what I have to do is accept that my story is part of me, allow myself to fully feel the pain of it, and then get on with the task of living the rest of the life I have.

Grenades and Guillotines

The grenade moment. Life has been trundling along and then, bang, with no warning, it explodes. Something makes your soul cry out, whacks you in the stomach with an iron bar, makes you feel that some outside agency has reached a fist into you, unfurling angry fingers and tearing your heart from your body. Life has changed forever; perhaps it feels unliveable.

Grenades come in all shapes and sizes. It might be a car crash or an accident, something that violently steals the life of a loved one. Or a diagnosis: the lump is no longer benign, the headaches and the nausea can't be fixed by taking more exercise and going on holiday. It could be a discovery: your partner loves someone else, or has been lying to you. The newspapers are full of other people's grenade moments. We see a terrorist attack, an earthquake, a flood, and know that we are witnessing the moment when everything changes. But somehow we don't believe that anything this dramatic will ever happen to us. 'I can't believe it,' is what we say when it does. 'It doesn't feel real. It's not fair.'

At school we had a large guillotine that was used to cut pieces of paper. We children weren't allowed near it unsupervised so there was a certain drama to watching it in action, the blade coming down and slicing the paper in two. That's what the grenade moment does. It separates the old life from the new and there will forever be a divide. The blade has come down. Life as we knew it has been detached, truncated. What lies on the other side is both unknowable and unthinkable.

When my grenade struck, the well-meaning grown-ups around me peddled the line that time is a great healer. And so, I waited to feel better, for life to return to normal. It never did.

What I now wish someone had told me is this: life will never be the same again. The old one is gone and you can't have it back. What you might at some point be able to encourage yourself to do, and time will be an ally in this, is work out how to adjust to your new world. You can patch up your raggedy heart and start thinking and feeling your way towards how you want to live. That's what I wish someone had told me and that's what I want to tell you.

There is a world on the other side of the guillotine. It's not the one you know and the undamaged version of you is lost in time. But there is a life to explore and a new version of you is waiting to walk into it.

An Etiquette Guide for Bad News

It seems ridiculous that in the face of someone else's misfortune we spend time worrying about our own behaviour, but it's only human and is particularly true when it comes to death and grief. I'm sure it was easier in Victorian times when there were prescribed rules, when society and the Church provided a framework. There was guidance on what to wear, how to communicate with people, how much time should elapse before everyone rejoined the business of life. Visible signs such as black crêpe and mourning brooches made of jet acted as clues to the rest of the world. Like a version of the 'Baby on Board' sign stuck in the back windscreen of a car, the blackness served as a warning that an individual needed to be treated kindly. All cultures have rituals around death and mourning but, in our increasingly secular society, it's easy to find ourselves unsure of what to do.

Having thought about it a lot and been on the receiving end of many different approaches, this is my attempt at an etiquette guide for bad news.

What to say

After much searching and thinking, I've realized there is no definitive piece of advice because it is impossible that any action of a friend or relative could make a newly grenade-struck person feel better. Perhaps the very essence of shock is that stunned feeling of being inconsolable.

But it helps to acknowledge it. This can be as simple as saying, 'I'm so sorry that this has happened to you.' The important thing is not to turn away, not to make people feel that their pain is unattractive or makes us uncomfortable. It's too easy to let fear of saying the wrong thing lead to not saying anything at all. Why is it so difficult to be near someone's distress? Do we want to make people feel better because we can't cope with witnessing their upset? Is it because of our modern tendency to refuse to accept that pain is part of life? Although, surely, our main worry is that we will say the wrong thing and make someone feel even worse.

I have come to see there is a beauty in simply being present for someone who is struggling with a heavy burden. The best thing you can offer is unlimited kindness. People to whom the worst has happened can be out-of-control sad and unable to obey the normal rules of life. It might be all they can do to hold on. If they are mean or cruel or temporarily incapable of good manners, we need to suspend our expectations around them and give them space and compassion as they splinter and behave badly and say the wrong thing. If they are behaving perfectly and holding themselves together, then that's OK, too. We don't need them to conform to our idea of how they should behave.

It's also worth thinking about timing. For instance, supporters are inclined to rally round in the immediate aftermath of a death with lasagnes galore, but then expect people to be fixed and sorted the day after the funeral. Grief is a long party, sadly, especially if the death has been out of the natural order of things. The initial bit is often fuelled with adrenaline and there's no shortage of people around – more flowers than there are vases to put them in. It's the later stages where help can mean more because there is less of it on offer. This is equally true of other situations, such as a diagnosis or a break-up.

But we don't need to over-assume responsibility. Nothing is going to make this person feel better because nothing can. There is no magic formula. People in distress may well take offence easily because they cannot be pleased. Our main duty is to let them and not take offence back.

One of the fascinating things about human beings is that we all view life differently and respond in wildly varying ways to the same event. Stress can make us long for others to behave as we would, when all we need to do is allow them space to be themselves. Some may want to talk and even joke, others to be left alone. Part of your job as a friend is to try to work out what they need and not worry too much about getting it wrong.

WHAT NOT TO SAY

I'm not generally in favour of negative instructions. The Internet is full of don'ts and I worry that we'll end up with such long lists of what not to say that we'll be forced into a place of resentful silence. That said, there are a few horrors I'd recommend avoiding:

Everything happens for a reason

I am not a violent person but being told this has always made me want to punch people in the face. It's an attempt to mould other people's distress into a belief system. If there is ever a time to seek meaning in tragedy – and I'm not sure there is – it certainly isn't in the immediate aftermath.

What doesn't kill you makes you stronger

This is presumably a well-meaning attempt to offer a silver lining but I've never liked being on the receiving end of it. I am unable to find any consolation in the fact that what happened to my brother resulted in an opportunity for self-development or personal growth for me. I also don't think it's true. For years, I felt like a pale version of the girl I might have been. I'd survived by the skin of my teeth but felt depleted rather than augmented by the experience. I wasn't more resilient; I didn't know whether I would survive another blow and I couldn't stop mourning my old self. I worried that with one more sad little straw, the exhausted camel's back would break.

God would not give you more than you can handle

How can anyone believe in the kind of God who sits up in the sky working out just how much tragedy and pain one person can take? There's a peculiarly passive-aggressive note to this. It looks like an attempt to console but feels like a criticism – if God would not give you more than you can handle, then any failure to handle it is your fault.

It comes to us all

This was said by her neighbour to a friend of mine who had just suffered a tragedy of biblical proportions. 'Does it?' she wanted to say. 'Does it?'

THINGS TO AVOID

Any sort of kicking off

In my years of being a barmaid I saw a lot of post-funeral arguments and humbly suggest that if you feel cross because of the way the service was organized, or how you were or weren't communicated with, you should try to give everyone the benefit of the doubt. No situation is improved by people squabbling over the venue for the wake, the policy around floral tributes, or the vexed question of who gets to carry the coffin or ride in the family hearse. Maybe just accept that no one will be at their best on a sad day and try to rise above it.

Getting carried away by your own sense of loss

This is tricky. It is obviously appropriate to acknowledge the qualities of the lost loved one and how much they meant to you, but resist the temptation to position yourself at the centre of everything. This happens at funerals when the next of kin end up acting as hosts and have to mop up the tears of those who are less closely affected.

Crossing the road

Telling someone that you are thinking of them with love, and offering practical help, is surely an improvement on crossing the road to avoid having to face them and find words.

Asking why they're worrying about it

With death and grief, we know the gravity of the

situation. When someone is struggling under a different burden, it's not helpful to tell them that their problem isn't as big a deal as they think it is. Always respect whatever is weighing on someone's mind.

Saying something just for the sake of it

Listening is important, something I often forget in my eagerness to try to make someone feel better, show them I understand, or offer practical advice they may not have thought of. A friend who volunteered for the Samaritans found the training in active listening useful for life. She wasn't there to judge or offer solutions, just to listen.

I like the notion of silent sympathy, which Bobbie from *The Railway Children* is good at. She knows when people are unhappy and makes them feel loved without having to tell them all the time how sorry she is for them.

Often people blunder into inanity or tactlessness because they are reaching for something, anything, rather than silence. Perhaps we need to accept that we don't have the power to fix anyone, but could just be there for them with love.

What to Do When the Worst Happens

Hold steady. Sadly, life's not fair. Sometimes there is no meaning or purpose to what happens to us or those we love. We can simply find ourselves in the wrong place at the wrong time. Don't ask, 'Why me?' but rather, 'Why not me?' It's cruel. It hurts so much. The pain is beyond anything you could ever have imagined.

Oh, I was angry with the people who tried to tell me about the five stages of grief. How could anyone know what I was feeling or try to reduce me and Matty and the uniqueness of my loss of him to a system? They made no sense to me, these stages. I didn't feel as though I was moving through a process. My grief wasn't linear. When I imagined it plotted on to the graph paper used to track Matty's temperature in hospital, it didn't show an upward gradient but a series of violent zigzags. Grief felt to me like an ever-extending roller coaster that dipped and swirled into new routes. Or a bucking bronco that might occasionally have a small rest before waking up with a vengeance, newly committed to trying to chuck me off its back.

Recently I decided to look up those stages and was expecting to see all the ways in which they are flawed. Instead, now that I'm no longer incapacitated by anger and confusion, I can see they aren't supposed to be interpreted as a one-size-fits-all, identikit plan, but can be a useful guide to some of the ways loss works upon us. Experiencing grief for the first time is like the dark twin of falling in love. It feels a bit crazy, and we don't think anyone has ever felt exactly as we do. But of course they have.

Denial, anger, bargaining, depression, acceptance. They didn't happen in much of an order for me, but I can now see that they are recognizable and relevant to any kind of loss. We don't want to believe it's happened, we're angry with a world that has allowed it to happen, we keep thinking of things that might have stopped it happening, we can't see any point or relevance to ever caring about anything else and then, finally, finally, we accept – not what has happened, but that life is still there to be lived.

If I could travel back in time and advise my younger self, I would not hide the fact that a whole new world of suffering had opened up, but I would encourage her to learn to recognize her urge to escape pain and try to resist it. There is nothing wrong or shameful in your distress, I'd say, and it will be better for you in the long run if you express it now. I promise it won't always feel like this.

I've never understood the notion of time being a great healer, because all I ever tried to do was grit my teeth and wait for time to pass or try to distract myself from it, but I missed the point. Time itself doesn't have magic properties; it's what you do with the time that matters. As my friend Dawn says, 'Time heals, but it's a slow fucker.'

Recently my mother told me something I never knew. After Matty was knocked over, she used to go alone down to the river, and there, on the banks of the Ouse, she would howl and howl. Then she would come back and get on with what needed to be done. She allowed herself to feel her anger, but did it in a way that didn't make things worse.

I couldn't bear to feel the pain of losing my brother, so I refused to allow time to do its work and was drunk for a decade. Then I stopped getting quite so drunk and started pouring my energy into work; and work, like alcohol, is not a bad way of refusing to sit with pain. Finally, I have stopped running away or drowning out my feelings and have allowed myself to become acquainted with the darker emotions of sadness, anger, fear and shame. And, with time, I have felt better.

The important thing to remember is that being upset over a loss or sadness is not an illness. It is part of being human. I used to be angry with grief and see it as a design flaw. I couldn't grasp the sheer scale of the mourning I'd done for Matty, couldn't see a purpose in those millions of tears.

When Matty and I were little and were trying to figure out the meaning of love, we decided that it meant you'd cry if someone died. And maybe that is it. I loved him, he died, and for years, I cried.

I have a new respect for grief and a new respect for myself as a traveller in it. I used to be frightened of loving people because I thought I wouldn't survive losing them, but now I see that making friends with grief, accepting it as part of being human, will liberate me to love even more, and that the love is always worth it.

I Am One in Four

In some cases loss and trauma can impact on our mental health. There isn't always a cause or trigger for mental health problems – it is perfectly possible to be mad without grief, mad because of grief or grieving without madness. For me, they have always felt linked.

According to the mental health charity MIND, one in four people will suffer a mental illness this year. Since finding this out I've been looking around me in social situations and wondering where they are.

Imagine a packed football stadium, a crowded street, the top deck of a full bus. Imagine if one in four of the people were sporting a big bandage wrapped around their head. You'd spot them immediately. If you had a bandage of your own, there would be plenty of other people with whom you could exchange sympathetic smiles, little flashes of empathy. Perhaps you could even compare bandage lengths and styles, ask them how they cope, if they've got any useful tips and tricks. But this one in four is often invisible. Each of us soldiers on alone thinking it's only us or 'properly' mad people, straitjacketed characters in films and literature, and the occasional celebrity spokesperson. We don't realize how common it is to experience a bout of mental ill health.

One in four is a huge number of people. It means that every one of us is closely connected to someone who struggles with their own mind. I think that's a reassuring thing to know. You are not alone. You are neither special nor terrible, you are just one in four.

I am one of the one in four. I had my first episode of depression when I was nineteen and I've been in and out of it ever since, with side helpings of anxiety and forays into panic attacks and psychosomatic illnesses.

People often ask me whether my mental health struggles are a direct result of what happened to my brother or whether I might have had problems anyway. It's a good question and I don't know the answer. I hadn't experienced depression before the accident but I was seventeen then; there wasn't much of me to know. When I was nineteen I was diagnosed with post-traumatic stress disorder, which has both depression and anxiety as its symptoms and would seem to fit the bill. Later, I thought this diagnosis must be wrong because surely it shouldn't keep carrying on. There must be something else, something different wrong with me.

It's tricky to write about depression. When I'm in it I see no point to anything so it's impossible to summon the necessary energy, and when it's over the whole thing has a strange dreamlike texture and I can't really remember it. I'm superstitious about it, too. I'm not sure I want to recall it well enough to write about it, because I don't want to remind myself of the feelings.

For me, depression is a dark, sludgy cocktail of lethargy, despair and futility. Other people talk of black dogs, but mine is all weather and weight. I'm surrounded by fog, mist, gloom, smoke and clouds. I feel heavy, and tied down, as though there are invisible weights strapped to my legs. Sometimes I feel pinched and bullied by disembodied wraith-like fingers that inject lead into my veins so my very blood is heavy. Other times I feel as though I'm suffocating, as though I've fallen face down into an enormous grey marshmallow and can't get up. Once I had a dream that I was at soft play with my son, Matt, but all the plastic balls were black and grey and I was buried under them and couldn't move or breathe.

When I'm depressed I can't even see a point to myself. I decide I'm a worthless person who has somehow tricked others into liking me and it is easy to believe that both my beloved son and the world at large would be better off without me. I have learned, though, not to allow myself to let this line of thinking drag me further downwards. 'This is just the depression,' I've learned to say to myself. 'Depression lies. Just hold on and wait for the wind to change and you won't feel this way any more.'

In the midst of it, all I want to do is cower under the bedclothes in a darkened room. And yet, if there is sufficient reason – being obligated to someone else, usually – I seem to have an override button that enables me to get up and out into the world. I always feel better when I'm on the move; it's getting moving that's the problem.

One of the ways I wait out the time is by listening to audio books under the covers and I've discovered that you can change the speed, increase or reduce it by either a quarter or a half. That's what I feel like. As though those smoky fingers have gained access to the motherboard of me, and keep turning me down, notch by cruel notch. It's not a binary state of affairs where

I'm either well or depressed. It's more like a staircase or a spiral. As my mood darkens, I feel like a toy running out of battery. My functionality is reduced.

Anxiety is a different beast. The last time it happened, I didn't clock it for a while, but thought I'd caught some kind of bug. I was on the verge of throwing up for several days, and it was only when my chest got so tight that I wondered if I was developing asthma, that I finally twigged. Ah, anxiety. It's deeply unpleasant but I don't fear it the way I do depression. I know I can grimly endure anxiety and loosen its grip by clean living and lots of exercise. It doesn't stop me being productive; rather the opposite, often heralding a frantic energy. I feel unappealing with it, sweaty palmed with a metallic taste in my mouth, convinced that my body smells sour. Unlike with depression, I always feel alive, even as I'm struggling for breath.

Thankfully, I no longer hyperventilate, and can usually breathe myself through and out the other side of panic attacks; the irritable bowel syndrome that plagued my twenties is a thing of the past. I was shocked the first time someone suggested to me that my physical symptoms might have psychological causes; but seeing a therapist, and exploring how guilty I felt that I was able to go out into the world when my brother couldn't, cured me after all the medical tests I'd had came up blank.

So why the secrecy? Why is there such a stigma? Why does admitting to all the above make me feel nervous, make me feel as though I'm coming out in a way that telling you about a bad back or a stomach ulcer wouldn't?

I lie all the time about how I'm feeling and always have done. Long before I experienced depression I was preoccupied with appearing normal. I wanted to fit in rather than stand out and didn't want to look peculiar. This emotional dishonesty skyrocketed when Matty was knocked over and it seemed obscene in the face of his great tragedy to ever complain about how difficult anything was for me.

I still seem stuck in this rut of believing that any distress I feel is ungrateful and indulgent. Now, with the ever-increasing awareness of global suffering enabled by twenty-four-hour news, I feel even more conscious of my good fortune. I was born to loving parents in a comparatively safe and prosperous part of the world and we always had enough to eat. I have a healthy child and do high-status and fulfilling work. I am mired in a deep shame at being unable to feel content.

I would never judge anyone else who suffered from depression – I understand that it isn't logical – but I deal myself a huge portion of self-loathing for my inability to simply be happy. I imagine the challenges faced by other mothers of small boys, what it must be like to be a refugee trying to take your children to safety, and I hate myself for not being able to appreciate my relatively fortunate situation more.

I'm frightened of talking about all this because I imagine shouty voices: 'First-world problems! What have *you* got to worry about?' I'm scared that, if I'm already full of self-loathing, I won't have enough energy to cope with other people's poor opinion of me and that my mood will spiral down and down and down until there is nowhere left to go.

Depression is difficult to explain, especially when we are in it. My usual linguistic abilities desert me as my brain fills up with cotton wool and my tongue feels fat in my mouth.

I once tried group therapy. There were eight of us sitting in a wide circle. The first thing we had to do was talk to the person next to us about why we were there. My partner was a man of about my age. I had to go first and I mumbled a bit about grief and then said I was there because someone had suggested that processing my pain might help with my tendency to depression. When it was his turn he told me that his wife had left him for someone else and wanted to move to the other side of the country with their two daughters. He'd poured everything into providing for them and couldn't understand why she didn't appreciate this. He wasn't sleeping. He just wanted everything to go back to normal. He stopped talking and looked at me. 'I bet you don't feel so bad about the depression now, do you?'

It took me a moment to realize what he meant, to see that he clearly viewed depression as a luxury ailment for those with no proper problems. He'd constructed a hierarchy of suffering and put me on the bottom rung. The main thing it showed me was that he'd never been depressed, because no one who had ever experienced it would try to compare it to anything else.

Pondering this little exchange afterwards, I felt it illuminated depression's catch-22. The more depressed you feel, the less able you are to communicate effectively and the more likely you are to be on the receiving end of something tactless or hurtful. I didn't feel particularly offended by this encounter because I wasn't actively depressed at the time, had plenty of good support in my life, and felt sorry for the man who was clearly flailing around, not understanding why his life was derailing; but what if that kind of response came from a parent, a lover, a friend or a boss? What if it was the first time I'd ever mentioned my depression out loud to anyone? Would I then feel belittled and disrespected and even more inclined to crawl under the covers and not come out again? I'm meant to be good with words, let's not forget, and I still find it all a minefield.

From a practical point of view, it's human instinct to hide any weakness from the rest of the pack. We want to appear competent so that we can do our jobs, look after our loved ones and survive. We want to be viewed as worthy and useful. This is why going out into the world as a member of the one in four is an act of bravery.

I first 'came out' by accident. I'd been talking on film for a video about the pleasures and benefits of reading. It was one of those things where you speak for ages on a range of themes and they only use a couple of clips.

As I watched myself on the screen say that reading was my only solace during dark times, that I found books easier to deal with than life, I realized that anyone with any knowledge of depression would know what I was talking about. After an initial surge of fear, I felt an odd sense of relief.

I like being on the record and think the benefits to me of feeling authentic and not having to expend all my energy on pretending to be other than I am are worth it, but, even among the one in four, I know I'm privileged to be 'high functioning', and to know that I am never a danger, or even an inconvenience, to anyone but myself. I am also lucky to work in the world of books. My industry is remarkably open-minded and tolerant. I was talking about this to a male friend who has a high-profile job in the City. He told me it would be unthinkable for him to let anyone he works with know about his OCD and anxiety. His career would be over.

This is so sad because the huge irony is that secrecy

over anything tends to add to the problem and compound our sense of shame. We don't want to embarrass people or make them feel worried or miserable, so we create a version of ourselves that we think they will want to see. We put all our efforts into projecting a false image rather than simply living as we are. And it makes us feel worse, partly because it takes so much energy to power up the false front that we have little left for anything else. If we don't think we are being real, it's easy to negate any affection from others. 'Ah,' says that horrid little voice in the ear. 'If only they knew what I was really like . . .'

When I decided to be honest about my anxiety, it immediately started to shift. A friend asked me how I was and I paused and, instead of saying, 'Fine,' said, 'Well, everything in my world is good and exciting and I know how fortunate I am, but my anxiety is off the chart and I haven't felt this crazy in years.' There was a moment when I thought, Will this person run away from me? But of course she didn't; she just smiled at me kindly and patted my arm, and I felt a tiny bit better. So, the next time someone asked me how I was, I tried it again, and they smiled at me and patted my arm, and I felt another tiny bit better.

The other day, I was doing a jigsaw with Matt, a beautiful thing with brightly coloured birds and animals, and I realized I feel a bit like a jigsaw. Sometimes I'm complete and sometimes I'm scattered around in pieces. As I kept checking the picture on the front of the box against the pieces we were arranging on the table, I thought again about authenticity and false fronts. I twigged that the less authentic I feel, the less connected I am to the image I'm projecting – what's on the front of the box of me – so the more difficult it becomes to keep myself together and the more likely it is that I will start breaking up.

Much of the language of mental illness is a language of disintegration. Cracking up, breaking down. Maybe a breakdown is almost more of a break-up. The break-up of the self.

We know that the worst thing to say to a depressed person is that they should pull themselves together; the problem isn't that it is bad advice, it's that we don't know how to do it. It has taken me over twenty years of getting depressed to realize that, for me, depression is a process of disintegration and reconstruction. My jigsaw scatters across the floor and then, eventually, I build myself anew.

I emerge from every episode feeling both different and stronger. I don't feel this when I'm in it – I don't think, Hooray, this is heralding a lovely period of self-development – can't wait to meet my new, upgraded self! but I can't now think of a single time when I didn't come out the other side feeling better than before, even though I didn't understand that at the time.

This is a new revelation and I'm curious and cautiously hopeful that this way of thinking might help me avoid the depths of depression in the future. Perhaps if I spent less of my energy on fear and more on paying attention to myself, I could focus on doing the often banal things that keep my mood in balance.

Coming out of depression can be gradual. Sometimes it is spectacular and there's a period of exhilaration, a bit like when you've had a really horrible cold with a stuffed-up nose and you remember how wonderful breathing is. When you come out of depression, as the fog lifts, you watch the grey world recolour itself. Everything is so full of promise. The skin of an aubergine is a work of art, the way a tin opener takes the lid off a tin is a magnificent feat of engineering. I want to run around, pointing at things. Isn't that clever? Isn't that beautiful? Aren't people kind?

I felt so good when I finished writing my first book that I allowed myself to fall into the trap of believing I was forever fixed. When this turned out not to be true it seemed more important than ever to find out what was wrong with me. If everything was due to the accident, and it really was post-traumatic stress disorder, then perhaps I could hope to one day be cured. Or, if there was a different diagnosis to be had, maybe there was a pill that could help me.

I poured effort into research, embarked on a frenzy of self-examination and interrogated my relatives about our family history. I learned lots of things along the way but, most importantly, that there are very few definitive answers. Different doctors and therapists have opposing opinions not only about me, but about everything to do with the causes of depression and how to treat it. Even the question of whether a tendency to experience mental health issues is genetic isn't easy to answer. There is no shortage of mental illness in my father's family – one of my cousins told me she has always thought of depression as our family curse – yet a lot of the sufferers led difficult lives and had big burdens. Who is to say their problems weren't post-traumatic rather than inherent?

One day, waiting for an appointment with the GP, I noticed that the room was packed with people who looked more in need of care than I did. I questioned why I was there. Yes, my depression had been lasting longer than usual but what was the point of me taking up the doctor's time, when lots of people were worse off? I was sitting next to a frail woman with sunken cheeks and no eyebrows, wearing a headscarf. I looked around at the grizzling children, the stressed parents, and the elderly people who had difficulty lowering themselves into and out of their seats, and felt full of shame. I wanted to run away. Then it suddenly occurred to me that I wouldn't be playing this comparisons game if I had a physical illness. If I had a broken leg, I wouldn't be berating myself because some people have had theirs amputated. Wouldn't it be good if we could think of our mental health as we do our physical health? Treat ourselves as we would if we had gout or hay fever?

I stayed for my appointment and cried all over my very good doctor, who was kind to me as she always is. She congratulated me on my self-management techniques, said I should continue my trauma therapy and told me to come back and never feel bad about taking up her time.

As I walked home, I decided to cease making a distinction between my mental and physical health. I have had a dodgy right ankle ever since I fell over on the library steps when I was twenty. I don't spend time agonizing about why I fell, or whether or not I had the best treatment; I just know that high heels aren't an option, skydiving probably isn't a sensible hobby and I wear an ankle-support bandage when I need it. None of this causes me any emotional anguish.

Perhaps it would be useful to start thinking about my mind as though it were my skin. I was the first person in my year at primary school to get acne, which earned me the nickname Spot. Thankfully, the name lost currency as everyone else caught up. Despite my early start, I never had the full-on condition that solicited soubriquets like Pizza Face or Crater Head. But it lasted all the same and has never fully gone away. I've had medical treatments but they didn't work or I didn't like the side effects. Over the years, I learned that people loved me despite my skin and I got better at looking after it. When it comes to skin, we understand that we are all different, that some people may need a dermatologist, some a bit of Clearasil and others might find benefits from less sugar and more fresh air.

This would seem a good way for us all to think about our mental health, whether or not we are one of the one in four. The mind is simply another part of the body. It works hard, deserves our care and we shouldn't feel ashamed about needing to give it some attention.

How to Feel Better

The big step for me in feeling better was accepting that I deserved to. I made a conscious effort to ditch the guilt and shame and then approached my well-being the way I would a work project, considering my options and thinking about who might be able to help me. I decided to seek some professional support and had a course of EMDR therapy, which stands for Eye Movement Desensitization and Reprocessing, and treats post-traumatic stress disorder. I found it helpful from the very first session and loved my therapist, who was full of wit and wisdom. EMDR was initially developed with army veterans. The idea is that during trauma we don't process memory properly and it gets stuck.

I know not everyone needs therapy or is lucky enough to have access to it, but it makes me sad that there are people who miss out on the benefits because they don't think it's for them. I'm happy to admit to having therapy – and I've had loads – if only to normalize the notion of it.

But there are other sources of help, too, and a key part in my quest to feel better was to approach everything with an open mind. After years of mocking mindfulness and meditation – I don't really know why – I have embraced them and they, alongside my therapy, have helped me to see how to manage myself. I treat my mind like an unruly toddler and don't let it get out of hand. My tone is kind but strict and I'm not allowing myself laziness or melodrama. I've learned to observe my thoughts, and have a little breathing space before translating them into damaging actions.

As with a staircase, things go up and down. The best aim for me is to try to stay on the middle steps. Too high, I'll go crashing off the top. Too low, I'll find it hard to get back up. I've moved from feeling frustrated that there are no good answers about depression to feeling liberated by the fact that no one really knows. Perhaps depression is unexpressed anger and sadness, and anxiety is fear gone out of whack. These days, I allow myself to feel sad and give space to darker feelings. I spend less time fighting depression and more time trying to make friends with it.

I have become less addicted to things. I've had periods of abstinence from alcohol, social media and news, which have further shown me how dangerous they all are to our well-being. I don't want to live in an ivory tower, so I am trying to work out how to have little bits of all of them. It's a funny bind with addictions. It seems that if you can take it or leave it, then it's fine to take it. If you can't, then you have to leave it.

What I'm really looking for in alcohol or any addiction is to escape pain, feel soothed and fit in. As my EMDR therapist says, 'We're mammals, we're wired for connectivity. Whether it's watching porn or playing tennis, all humans are constantly seeking to connect.' This helped me see how I like the three-drink feeling when I am pleasantly anaesthetized and everyone around me starts being honest about themselves. In a flash of inspiration I clocked that I can desire alcohol less if I don't wait for it to give me permission to have meaningful conversations. These days, I'm diving from small talk into big talk without the encouragement of a few drinks and enjoying knowing that we are all just little pieces in the massive puzzle of humanity. We like to feel as though we fit in with everything around us.

When I feel the urge to do something I'm addicted to, I imagine I'm a dog looking at a rabbit. I used to bound off in pursuit the moment I saw it in the distance. Now, I can acknowledge that my ears have pricked up, but I can take a few breaths, or do something else, and think carefully about whether or not it really is worth chasing the rabbit today.

I've become more aware of my personal triggers. Being hungover reminds me of being depressed – the lethargy, the queasiness, the longing for it to be over – and this knowledge helps me stay more or less on the straight and narrow when it comes to booze. Being frightened reminds me of having anxiety – the racing heartbeat, the shortness of breath – so I'm careful about not watching or reading scary things that set me off. If I'm physically ill or cold for long periods of time then my mood dips, and there is no point in giving any airtime to my gloomy mental chatter if I have allowed myself to get too tired or too hungry. It's so simple but so powerful to be aware of when I shouldn't listen to my thoughts, but should concentrate on looking after myself instead.

Is modern life rubbish? Certainly it is full of luxuries and challenges that our forebears could not have begun to imagine. I like to picture my cave-people ancestors sitting around a fire. The stresses they were exposed to were considerable, no doubt, but they didn't have all the cruelty of the world only a click away. They weren't able to see the last texts people sent their mums when they knew they were about to die, or watch the final moments of a man shot by police, and hear his girlfriend's sobs as the life drained out of him. They didn't have social media, with its bright lights administering bursts of dopamine to frazzled brains. They didn't have the noise, the sense of overwhelm, or people popping up to tell them they were pointless, or untalented or trashy or wrong. We are not designed to have all of this delivered into our hands on a screen that we carry around with us and which is always on.

Looking back at the times in my life when I broke down, I see that watching the twin towers fall again and again and gluing myself to reports of houses being washed away in Japanese floods were contributing factors to my disintegrating state of mind. It seems ghastly to refuse to bear witness to other people's tragedy because I'm such a delicate flower, but I have to see that it does the world no good if I can't manage to live in it.

One thing I know for sure about myself is that my empathy levels are set high. I catch other people's joy and distress by osmosis. This is useful for mind reading and writing but I need to be careful about not over-loading myself. Perhaps we all do. Vicarious trauma is the expression used to describe what can happen to caregivers, to those working on the front line with tragedy and suffering. Watching and reading too much news is potentially exposing us all to vicarious trauma, and we aren't designed to cope with the onslaught as channels compete for our attention in the aftermath of a global tragedy. To stay sane, I need to maintain a faith in humanity and this is hard to do when staring at screens.

If I'm feeling overwhelmed at the state of the world, then social media pushes me further into impotent rage and misanthropy where I can mistake being cross about something for actually taking action. If I'm feeling anxious, social media amplifies it. It can feel like a big party, but it can also feel like a big party to which I haven't been invited. Fear of not fitting in can be even more potent than fear of missing out and I'm astonished how often it makes me feel as though I am back in the playground or not being picked for the rounders team.

If I'm having any sort of identity struggles then social media is just too confusing as, by nature, it is fragmented and inauthentic. It used to be that only famous people experienced what it felt like to look beautiful on a billboard and miserable inside. Now anyone with a social media profile is at risk of what I have started to think of as 'avataritis' – the authenticity dilemma of having our complex selves represented by a single image and a collection of status updates. I like Facebook because I enjoy being in touch with friends and relatives and seeing pictures of their kids and pets but I'm always aware that I'm showing a highly select-ive slice of my life. I post a picture of Matt looking adorable, and not one of me, later that same afternoon, sobbing in despair over what a useless mother I am after yet another squabble over homework. I've made lots of friends on Twitter but when I got to the point where I'd tweet something innocuous and then instantly delete it because I was scared of what people might say, I realized it was time to put it down for a while.

If a cavewoman encountered a reproving eyebrow-raise from one of her small community, it would usefully make her think twice about her actions, but surely none of us has evolved sufficiently to cope with online censure? I rather like being disagreed with in real life – I don't think I'm always right and enjoy having my ideas tested – but I can't cope with it online. I'm not sure why it feels so brutal. Perhaps it's the absence of eye contact, or the spectre of an unseen audience, but I find it anxiety-inducing. I'm filing it under a long list of things I don't fully understand but accepting that, for me, especially in low mood, online life can be kryptonite.

I have drawn back from the modern dilemma of thinking I have to have an opinion about everything. I'm making efforts to be less reactive, to stop finding fault with things. I am trying to note the existence of irritating people, sexist taxi drivers and malfunctioning printers without taking to Twitter to protest about them or allowing them to knock me off course. I think of it as reversing. When I realize something isn't good for me, I don't have to understand why, or be judgemental about it; I can just reverse out. It's a liberating notion. I'm thinking of reversing out of having a smartphone, reversing out of the need to be informed, reversing out of taking offence.

I've opened up a bit, and it's helped to think of this as nurturing my mental health, rather than admitting to mental illness. When people ask why I'm not drinking – yes, all of society prefers me inebriated, it seems – I say, 'I find it's better for my mental health to have time off.' When they ask about my absence from social media, I say the same thing. I imagine myself as a big battery. Sometimes I'm fully charged and sometimes running low. If my energy levels are starting to drop, I need to plug in to a source.

Years ago, I was taught some exercises to stop me hyperventilating but it didn't occur to me that learning to breathe would be of wider use. Now I have fallen blissfully in love with my own breath. Breathing is a superpower. It's an incredible way to calm down and I can breathe myself out of cravings.

I'm trying to cease the pursuit of perfection and to expect less of myself as a person, as a mother and as a writer. It's OK for me not to have answers to everything, to be impatient with my child when he is kicking off and to feel apprehensive about putting words into the world. There will be people who won't like me and my work but I can live with that. It only matters if the fear of it stops me doing anything at all.

I was humming Nina Simone to myself one day when I realized that I have to be better at tolerating the prospect of being misunderstood, because it will happen and there is nothing I can do about it. At least I know my intentions are always good.

I've also learned to laugh at myself a little. Writing down my fears and worries is really good for me because my lists start with all the big questions of life and trickle down into rather sweet nonsense. Right at the top is global injustice and everyone I love dying horribly but by the time I reach the bottom of the page I'm obsessing about being a bad mother; or not liking my appearance; or feeling wound up about the state of my inbox, the kitchen or how much ironing there is to do. I allow a bit of this feeling sorry for myself and then I start to find my catastrophizing a bit funny.

I've known for a while that writing a list of things I'm grateful for is helpful and now I understand why. Our minds are designed to scan for danger and risk, not for good things. By making a list, we are jumping tracks on to a more positive train of thought. It's hard to do at first, but if I stick with it, it works. This morning's list included the fact that my parents are coming to stay tomorrow, that I've made chicken soup from scratch and that I can see a beautiful tree from my window.

I am trying to love my body more, appreciate the way it carries me around, and stop subjecting it to alternate regimes of austerity and indulgence. How sad that I have spent such a ludicrous amount of time wanting there to be less of me. The scales are gone. I've listened to Nora Ephron, who said that everything you dislike about your body at thirty-five, you'll feel nostalgic for at forty-five. I absolutely know that when I'm on my deathbed I won't wish I'd spent more time trying to be thinner. Anyway, I doubt that over-consumption has anything to do with greediness and willpower, but is all about not wanting to feel pain. I will never make another resolution that involves depriving or reducing myself. Maybe one of the reasons January is miserable is because no one is eating enough.

I try not to let feeling powerless to alter the state of the world stop me from doing little things that might make it better, even if only for one person for a tiny amount of time. I like to embrace my inner Pollyanna and it always helps me to do something for someone else. 'Social glow' is the rather wonderful term for the warm feeling that comes from being useful to our fellow humans. I like to be alive to the possibility of offering help, which might be as simple as carrying a buggy up the stairs, opening the door for someone or coming to the rescue of lost tourists.

There are lots of charities with one-off donation schemes, where you can pay for a bed at a homeless shelter or a package from Refuge, and my supermarket has a collection area for the local food bank. When Matt's school send home forms asking for money for school trips, they also offer the opportunity to sponsor another child. I love to do this. I can easily afford to, but I like to think I'd do it even if it was more of a struggle. It's a tiny drop in the puddle of the world's injustice, but it also helps me to see that things have moved on in some ways. My dad's main memories of school are of being humiliated for being poor and dirty, being beaten for not paying attention and feeling abandoned on school trip days when all the wealthier children went off to Kerry and he was left alone. I'm glad that isn't happening to any of Matt's classmates.

These days I am offered opportunities to be helpful and useful and I try to take them by chairing charity events, mentoring people and doing prison visits, but I often think about what I could do if I was poor in money and time. A really simple thing is to always be nice to waiters and shop assistants. People in service industries have to suffer the anger of everyone who isn't good at appropriately directing their frustrations. After years of selling booze and books and knowing that sometimes customers were shouting at me because they couldn't shout at the person they were really angry with, I can tell you that being courteous and respectful towards whoever is selling or serving you something is a moral act. If you happen to witness a bit of bullying in a customer service environment then a sympathetic smile or eyebrow-raise to the person bearing the brunt of it will be appreciated.

I've always loved books and reading, and ferreting out the life lessons hidden in everything from the Stoics to Narnia. Recently I'd been reading the Roman philosopher Seneca when Matt came home from school and told me about the YOYOB chart. It stands for 'You Own Your Own Behaviour' and the children get various stages of warnings before having their much-anticipated Friday-afternoon privilege time taken away from them in five-minute instalments. 'You own your own behaviour' is essentially the Stoic message. No matter what happens, we always have dominion over ourselves.

I'm trying to walk my own line, with two feet in my own life. Sometimes I love stepping out into the world, other times it is as much as I can do to put one foot in front of the other.

When my mood dips, I retrench, look after myself

and know that the future me will be grateful that I didn't make things worse. No point in worrying about it now, I think. Just add it to the list for when the wind changes. When I'm better, troubles that seemed insurmountable are usually simple either to deal with or to accommodate.

Despite everything I've learned, I still long to feel fixed, to be a blank page, a fresh canvas. There are all sorts of things I wish I didn't know. Like Eve, already regretting munching the apple, I'd like to be able to reject knowledge and experience, to wave a wand, turn back time, refuse to accept that what happened really happened. But even so, I know that it is much better for us to learn to wear our experiences with pride.

In *The Last Act of Love* I wrote about 'kintsugi', the Japanese style of ceramics where a broken object is mended in an intentionally obvious way. Rather than try to hide the cracks, the potter works with gold to show us that the breakage will always be there and has become an acknowledged – and beautiful – part of the object's history.

I've always loved this idea. We don't need to be unbroken. Our first step is simply to stop trying to hide our scars. Heartache is human.

Of course, part of the reason I long to be fixed is because I am frightened that I will get depressed again, and that next time it might be worse. The mean voice in my head, the one I'm doing such a brilliant job of not listening to, shouts at me from time to time, 'Ha, you think you've got it sussed with all this Pollyanna shit but it's not your brilliant techniques, you idiot, it's that you weren't that bad last time! You were only in mild-to-moderate territory, not severe. You'll never cope in the future. You'll never cope with a PROPER BURST.'

Thank you, mean voice, I say, for reminding me that there is a tension between being mindful of my mental health and being in a constant state of vigilance where I feel there is no pleasure in anything because I'm braced, just waiting for the day when I wake up feeling worse.

Recently, I decided to make a plan of action for the future while I'm well, so that I know I've done all I can. And then I can get on with enjoying the view from the middle of the staircase.

Instructions to My Future Self

My dear, my dear,

Somewhere in the future you are in a bit of a pickle. Please accept lots of love. Perhaps something horrible has happened to you or the world or perhaps you are just tired out. It doesn't matter. The main thing is that you are in a muddle and all of your usual skills and abilities have deserted you. I am here to help.

The first thing I want you to remember is that this is a temporary state of affairs. I know it's horrible but it won't last. You've been here before and you will survive it this time, like all the others. I promise you that in your future you are glad to be alive.

Now, we are going to reboot.

Here's what I want you to do:

— Stop drinking alcohol. Don't waste any time worrying about whether you have to stop drinking forever, just stop drinking now.

— If you have anxiety symptoms, you need to stop drinking caffeine too.

— Stop watching and reading the news and take the social media apps off your mobile. Turn your laptop and phone off by 7 p.m. and don't look at them again until morning. No matter what is happening in the world, you won't serve it by spinning out of control.

— If you are on any kind of diet, stop. The only dietary rule you are allowed to follow is a general aim to drink lots of water, eat lots of vegetables and not have too much sugar. Please try to stop giving yourself a hard time about being lazy or fat or ugly. You're not.

— Cry. If you don't want to dwell on events in your

own life then read sad books. Give in to tears. Think of it like bleeding a radiator.

— Every morning, first thing, write from your deepest, darkest, most shameful place. Get the things you are most worried about or frightened of down on paper and tell yourself it's better off out than in.

— Then remember Nancy Mitford, who said that life was often dull and sometimes sad, but there are currants in the cake. Look for the currants. Every day, write down five things you feel grateful for. You won't want to do this because you won't feel grateful for anything, but it's important. It can be simple things like being warm, having clean air to breathe and water to drink, or being able to afford vitamin pills. You could list your friends, or times when people have been kind.

— Read gentle, comforting, funny things. Try to laugh or, if you can't do that, feel amused. Don't read or watch anything scary or disturbing until you feel better.

— Try to be curious and interested in your experience.

— I know you won't think you have enough energy to do any of this, but if you can, try to get outside and walk, swim, look up at the sky, do some yoga. That will all help and is especially important in winter.

— Cook. Roast an organic chicken and make stock. If this feels too much, make a plain omelette and serve it with some salad.

— Be as honest as you can with the people around you.

— Ask for help. Who can help you?

— Cuddle.

— Hold on.

If you do all the above, I'd expect you to feel a tiny bit better after a couple of days and significantly better after ten. Mark the date. If you experience two weeks of full-on despair then go to the doctor.

Other than the above, don't try to change anything.

Don't make any decisions. Your entire world view is bleak at the moment so there is no point in trying to apply logic to life. Keep up with your commitments if you can, but otherwise just hold on.

Future you – future us, I guess – will be glad you didn't do anything but take care of yourself and wait for the wind to change.

Future you will be so pleased and proud that there is less mopping-up to do these days. Future you is really impressed with your management skills. We both send you lots of love and the absolute knowledge that things will be OK.

Remember, my darling, you are not particularly unusual – you are simply one in four.

Emotional Time Travel

Since I stopped treating time like the enemy, I've started to have a bit of fun with it and have invented a new game I call 'reclaiming'. The first success I had was with rain. Rain has often been present when things have gone awry with me, and I began to suspect it was a contributing factor rather than a coincidence. I've learned that when faced with any situation, our brains start scanning for previous experiences so that we know how to respond to this new challenge. This was helpful when we needed to know what to do when a tiger hove into view, less so in a world where we are continually bombarded with stress and stimulation. This is how we get triggered. I realized that when I sit and stare at the rain, my mind starts up a slideshow of all my previous breakdowns and pretty soon my mood is dipping because all I'm doing is remembering miserable episodes. I decided to see if I could rewire my brain.

We were in Cornwall, where it really does know how to rain. On one incessant day, I asked Matt if he fancied going outside to play. We'd get completely soaked but would have loads of fun. He was up for it and we abandoned ourselves to rolling in the grass, playing football, and running around trying to keep warm. Afterwards, we ran a hot bath and got in it together and read *Horrible Histories – The Tudors* before wrapping ourselves up in warm, clean towels. All the way through I kept willing myself to remember it, actively capturing happy rain-soaked images.

Now, when it rains, I no longer think about going mad, but picture Matt's wet and rather grubby face. I can see his damp eyelashes, and the bit of tree bark clinging on to his cheek. I can smell the wet Cornish grass. I have reclaimed the rain.

A few months later, I was in Dublin for a literary festival. It rained so hard that my only shoes – an already rather scruffy pair of red Converse – were soaked through and smelly. Around the corner from my hotel, I found a lovely big shop called Dunnes and was making my way to the shoe department when I saw the most magnificent mini wellies, grey with white and yellow daisies, for 15 euros. They needed no breaking in and I skipped around Dublin and then London during our very rainy summer and it was astonishing how much they cheered me up.

Now, when it rains, my mind considers playing the misery slideshow from hell, but instead chooses to focus on Matt's dear little face and to think, Oh, it's raining, I can wear my flowery wellies.

A similar mental process seems to happen around anniversaries. Significant dates punctuate the calendar like hurdles to be scraped over or crashed into. I have actively not committed the dates of my brother's death or funeral to memory. His birthday and the date of the accident are burnt on my brain and I've never wanted additional days on which to feel more than usually bereft.

It has helped me to accept that it is better to give in to the sadness than to fight it. Now, on my brother's birthday and the date he was knocked over, I accept that I will be preoccupied with thoughts of him and think it's fitting to spend some time in remembrance and tribute. I allow myself to feel the loss but also take care to remember him as he was, rather than snagging myself on memories of my own distress. From now on I will spend Matty's anniversaries honouring him and his memory. He is and always will be a part of my jigsaw and I've decided it's better to give some dedicated time to grieving him.

It's quite something to realize that you can have power and influence over your own thoughts and moods. This is so important, as the terror of depression is that it might descend unbidden at any moment. Having thought it all through calmly, I decided to see where else I could make a change.

I reclaimed the first and last moments of every day. All that half-awake time was full of stress and worry and I was often reaching for my phone before I'd rubbed the sleep out of my eyes. I deliberately decided to fill this time with gratitude instead. I think of five things I'm grateful for before going to sleep and the same when I wake up. My bedroom is a phone-free zone and I think carefully about when I am ready to invite the world into my space.

Sometimes reclaiming can be as simple as interrogating myself and rebranding long-held beliefs that might not be doing me any good. Last Monday Matt's school was having an anti-bullying awareness day, where they discussed how it is important to be an upstander rather than a bystander. The children were encouraged to wear blue mufti and were told that the colour's name stands for 'Be Lovely and Understanding to Everyone'. It made me consider how much I used to hate Mondays when I had various horrible jobs, and how I'm still stuck in this way of thinking even though my working days no longer follow the same weekly structure. I resolved that from now on I would reclaim Mondays by using them to remind me of this lovely group of kids being taught by dedicated and imaginative teachers that kindness and tolerance rule.

Were there other things that I could reclaim? I thought about the way we speak of depression as a struggle, a fight or a battle. And all those words do accurately describe how I have considered my relationship with depression for more than twenty years. However, when I decided to rebrand 'battling with depression' as 'dancing with my mood', I almost immediately felt lighter and less tense.

Words matter. I was talking to a dear friend struggling valiantly with many burdens and noted the horrible language she was using about herself. Idiot . . . useless . . . fuck-up . . . pointless. I begged her to stop and since then have tried not to use angry words about myself or anyone else.

I keep an eye out for people and things that make me feel bad and then try either to avoid them or to protect myself more. I trust my instincts and try not to over-think everything. Instead I ask myself how something makes me feel. I don't fully understand why social media plays with my head so much, but I don't need to. I only need to know that when it makes me feel angry, aggressive and judgemental I should put it down.

The good news about triggers is that we can create positive ones, too. I call these talismans, which means an object with magical properties, but they can be anything that reminds us of something good, like my flowery wellies.

Lots of mine are gifts. A lobster fridge magnet that fills me with joy, a necklace shaped like a piece of puzzle, a mug, some badges, a bookmark . . . I love that you don't need much money to do this. Feathers, stones and leaves are excellent talismans. Sometimes they develop over time. Matt decorated my laptop with Star Wars Lego stickers. At first I didn't especially notice them. Then I started to be amused by the quizzical looks I'd get when working in a cafe. Gradually I became more and more attached to my Lego Princess Leia and the instant jolt of love I'd get, especially far from home, when thinking of Matt just before getting down to work. We turn our noses up at fridge-magnet wisdom but I've come to enjoy scribbling down quotes I find on to various designs of pretty Post-it notes and dotting them around me.

I also keep a memory box, which I think of as storing up treasure for when I'm old. Letters, cards, receipts even – anything that reminds me of something good. I like to imagine myself as an old lady, my wrinkled hands reaching out for objects that will allow me to travel back through time and remind me what it was like to be alive now.

I look for ways to help me stay in this moment rather than obsessing over the sadness of the past or peering frantically into the future, trying to guess what terrors it holds and the myriad ways in which I fear I will fail to cope.

Should we try to live each day as our last? I used to struggle with this as I couldn't make it fit with the attempt to lead a well-ordered, balanced life. I thought that I needed the notion of future and consequences to keep a leash on my behaviour, making sure I aimed for a larger meaning and purpose than the pursuit of immediate pleasure. Now I like playing around with the idea. I would no longer want to spend this mythical final day in an orgy of excess, but would want to express appreciation and wonder for what I have known.

We remember our last normal day with intensity. I remember bits of the day before my brother's accident as vividly as if they had all happened this morning. Often grenade-struck people say they wish they had realized how happy they were, and while I don't want something terrible to happen tomorrow, I do like the idea of trying to lay down long-term memories of the brilliantly banal pleasures of my everyday life as it is now. It doesn't really work to try to do it with the whole day – there's too much going on – but I can decide to give my full attention to a part of it.

The other day I had an invigorating meeting and as I kissed my lunch date goodbye, breathing in her perfume, the scent of her face powder, I decided to really concentrate on my onward walk rather than dive into my phone. I strolled off through Soho, passing a man in chef's whites who was smoking a cigarette in the doorway outside a restaurant on Archer Street. I noted the detail of the bricks. I walked down Shaftesbury Avenue past the portrait painters, allowing myself to remember my friend at university who used to have a pitch there in the summer. He was from Uganda and I wondered what had happened to him, where his ambitions to be an artist had taken him. Then I crossed Piccadilly Circus, where there was an incredibly handsome young man playing the bagpipes, and I watched the tourists gathering round him and the joyous way the music combined with the traffic. And I continued down Piccadilly, looking at the books in the windows of Waterstones and then Hatchards, both shops I once worked in, and allowed myself to be flooded with memories of those times. When I arrived at Green Park Tube station I felt that the twenty minutes or so it had taken me to walk from one place to the other had been well spent, so I wrote it all down on the Tube on my way home. This is a gift I try to give myself every so often: a moment of thinking, Let me try to intensely remember this, let me try to intensely remember what it was like for me to be alive on this day.

The notion of proxy is something I learned in my therapy. We are inclined to be very hard on ourselves, far less compassionate than we would be with others. We can sometimes shift this judgement by imagining what we would say to a friend who was beating themselves up over the same thing that we can't forgive ourselves for. Now, rather than looking back on the unwise actions of my younger self with disdain, I feel as though I can reach back through the years with sympathy and love.

One day I came up with the idea of buying my seventeen-year-old self a present. I wondered what she would have most liked to own, if someone had offered her a gift on that last normal day. She liked books, reading, clumpy shoes and charity-shop clothes, especially cardigans. Her favourite colours were purple and green. I imagine sitting in her bedroom, watching her tie purple and green ribbons into her henna-red hair on the night before everything changed. I see that I can't save her from anything, I can't stop what is about to happen, but I can be grateful to her for getting through it so that we could arrive together in our current world full of lovely and interesting people, books and reading, and green cardigans galore. She survived, and it has amused me to buy a pair of purple Doc Marten shoes and wear them for her as I carry on stepping out into our life.

On Being a Hopeful Agnostic

Matt joined the Beavers when he turned six. There are boys and girls and they meet in a Scout hut and run around looking cute in turquoise outfits. When Matt joined, he had to learn the Beaver Promise and we had a fair few discussions about the fact that it includes a bit about loving God.

'But I don't believe in God,' he said.

'I don't believe in God either,' I said. 'But I can say prayers if we go to church for weddings and funerals. I don't think it harms anyone for me to join in a bit. It's up to you.'

Eventually he decided to say it.

Recently we all went up to Leicester for the

christening of my second cousin. I call these children – the children of my dear cousins Ralph and Simon – 'the cousinettes'.

On the way, Matt was working out all the connections.

'So, my only first cousins are my Dutch ones because your brother died without having children. Is that right, Mummy?'

My heart flinched and my mind tried to fly into sorrow. I took a breath.

'That's right, darling. But you have lots of second cousins, because you are related to all the children of my cousins.'

In the church, I followed along with the prayers as Martha, a very happy and chilled-out baby, was welcomed into God's love.

The priest talked about how to live, how to do service. He said, 'Don't underestimate the effect one good and God-loving person can have on this world.'

I thought about this. So much about religion

appeals to me. I loved the Catholic school I went to and RE was one of my favourite subjects. I often enjoy novels featuring religion and I loved learning about the five pillars of Islam via Matt's school project. I tend to be drawn to believers, and find them interesting. I like the notions of gathering as a community, singing together, giving thanks, accepting our failings, welcoming babies into the world and bidding farewell to those who have died, with respect and ritual.

I've always been drawn to the idea of confession and used to rather envy my Catholic classmates when they went off to see the visiting priest, not only because it meant they got out of double maths. I feel it would suit me. My dad, still smarting from his experiences growing up in Catholic Ireland, thinks it is just the way for the priest to know everyone's business, but I can see the appeal of rocking up every week, sharing my woes about succumbing to mean and petty behaviour, and feeling cleansed.

I like churches: their sense of history, the knowledge that so many humans have walked on their stone floors. I've taken to lighting a candle for my brother. I like to watch his flame flicker among all the others, to think of him in a community of lost loved ones, to think of me in a community of the bereaved. There are functions of religion that our secular society has not worked out how to replace, perhaps especially around death and grief.

I've often wondered whether this interest is part of a long courtship that will end in observance. Will I one day transform from a hopeful agnostic into a true believer? My main barrier is not so much believing in God but in having to pick a team. How can anyone, including the atheists, be so sure they are right?

I read an article about people with missing siblings. A large proportion of them had found God since their loss. I begrudge no one any comfort, and sometimes feel my own yearning to succumb to a higher purpose, but it's not an urge that I trust.

I ascribe any spiritual yearnings in myself, anything that would involve believing in the possibility of an afterlife or communicating with the dead, as an attempt to construct my own magic mirror, and I don't think it would do me any good.

In the end, I think that if you take God away from what the priest said as Martha gurgled at him, it still works. When we are bowed down by the state of the world, we should not forget the positive effects of trying to move through it as a good person.

What I've come to see is not that things happen for a reason, but that there is some sort of trick whereby you can look at your mangled wreckage and from it craft meaning and purpose. My favourite bit in all of Shakespeare is a line from *The Merchant of Venice* about a candle throwing its beam: 'So shines a good deed in a naughty world.'

This has always been helpful when I've been

struggling with the vastness of this cruel world. When everything seems so broken that my own actions feel pointless, I tell myself that I can't do anything about the naughty world, but I can decide to be a good deed. And then I think that even this is a bit too much and decide I'm going to be a fucked-up and flawed but basically well-intentioned deed. And if I sail forth with that in mind, I should be OK.

I now understand why I'm so interested in religion. It isn't anything to do with God; it's to do with people. Religions, all of them, are coping strategies. They're people trying to find explanations, rationalize their existences, deal with pain, and work out how to live.

I read somewhere that you can't cherry-pick from religion, but in my view that's absolutely what you should be able to do. Cherry-pick away. There's lots of wisdom, insight and magnificence in all religions – people have been pouring their energies into them for thousands of years. From now on, I'm going to pluck whatever fruit I like whenever I see it and stop over-thinking it all. If I am comforted by going into a church and lighting a candle, so be it. If I want to write up Buddhist sayings and stick them on the fridge, that's fine too. I used to feel an urge to pray for people but couldn't work out how to do it, because I thought I had to make a decision about who to pray to. Now I simply take some quiet time to wish my fellow humans well without needing the intermediary of a God.

One of the things I get from being in a church is that it makes me feel small in a good way. Recently I read a novel called *To the Bright Edge of the World* by Eowyn Ivey. One of the characters is a museum archivist who lives in Alaska. He spent a short time in Vancouver but didn't like it. He explains that Alaska makes him feel small in a good way, but Vancouver made him feel small in a bad way.

Aha, I thought, that's a secret of life. It helps for us to feel small in a good way. Some of the things that do this for me are reading books; being by the sea and watching the tide flow in and out; old buildings and museums; lying on the grass and staring up at the sky through the branches of a tree; and walking in the dark while looking up at the stars.

Some things that make me feel small in a bad way are the news, social media, busy roads, roundabouts, rush-hour traffic and advertising. Lots of these are necessary – it isn't about eradicating them, but about understanding and mitigating their effects.

Perhaps my spiritual yearnings would be fulfilled by making sure I spend plenty of time feeling small in a good way. This is how I feel when I pick Matt up from Beavers. I like to get there early to watch the end of the crab football or four-way tug of war – whatever their final letting-off-steam game is – and to see this bunch of tiny, noisy humans make the Beaver Promise.

'I promise that I will do my best, be kind and help-ful, and love God.'

As at the christening, I often reflect that since the God bit can be optional, it's not a bad distillation of how we could all seek to live.

The Last Piece of the Puzzle

There is a final piece to be placed into the jigsaw of the story of my brother and his sister. I'd like to share it with you here.

Matty died in 1998 and there was a big funeral but, as far as I remembered, we were never able to face the final stage of picking up his ashes from the undertaker. I fretted about this over the years but didn't want to ask my parents about it, partly because we all avoided the subject of Matty for fear of causing each other pain, but also because I didn't trust my memory. I had been anguished and out of control after the funeral. What if there had been some kind of ceremony that I'd blotted out because I'd been so mad and drunk?

In the course of writing my first book I finally asked my mother. She told me that we hadn't collected them, and that they were safely held at the undertaker's in Yorkshire, along with other uncollected urns, some going back fifty years. A friend who works as a bereavement counsellor told me it isn't uncommon for ashes to remain unclaimed, especially in the case of a difficult and untimely death. We weren't the only ones who'd been unable to clear the final hurdle. Once again I felt a poignant solace in not being alone.

Now, my parents and I felt it was time and after many slow, cautious conversations we decided to scatter Matty's ashes in the sea at Falmouth and then have a small slate plaque placed on my granny's grave in Swanpool cemetery.

My granny chose and bought her plot several years before she died. It's near her parents' and she'd go to tend their grave and then spend time sitting by her own future resting place, looking out over the sea. I was fond of my granny and thought of her as an old lady, though she was only fifty-nine when she died. It seems a young age to have put so much thought and planning into death, but she had already had one bout of cancer and my granddad had died four years earlier, after his second heart attack, so perhaps that had concentrated her mind.

We thought of burying Matty's ashes in the grave itself, but it didn't feel right to incarcerate him again, after he'd spent so long in a persistent vegetative state. I wanted him to be free and unfettered and liked the notion of casting him to the winds, so that he would settle into the sea that had delivered our father to his first chance meeting with our mother on Custom House Quay in 1968.

I had imagined collecting Matty from Yorkshire myself and escorting him down to Cornwall by train or car, but in the end this seemed too eccentric, or too logistically difficult, or some fiendish combination of both.

By Christmas, we were ready. Or were we? The

stonemason in Penryn had not returned our call and that seemed to be a sufficient reason to delay. My mother told me the ashes had been delivered but I didn't know where in the house they were. The apple loft? The long cupboard? The shed? I desperately wanted to know but was afraid to find out.

I didn't feel great. I wasn't in a big depression; I could function, but felt slow and clunky and unable to take pleasure in anything. I wanted to be able to appreciate being with my family and feel glad that I was in Cornwall for Christmas, but I couldn't conjure up much in the way of spark.

On Christmas Eve I went into Truro and did some writing in the Waterstones cafe. Then I bought a pasty from Rowe's and ate it sitting on a bench outside the cathedral before venturing inside. I walked around and found the area where you can light a candle. Tea lights, small and squat, with a suggested price of a pound. I paid the money into the metal box, lit my candle from another and placed it with its fellows. There must have been over a hundred flickering lights. I looked at the flames and thought of all the people in Truro who would head in here today to light candles for lost loved ones. I watched a man and woman light one together. Something in the way they held themselves was fragile, and made me think their loss was recent. I sat down and quietly cried, for them, for everyone, for myself.

On Christmas Day we built Star Wars Lego and went into Falmouth, where we walked along the seafront to watch the swimmers off Gyllyngvase beach. It was a sunny day and Matt wanted to go in, so I let him strip down to his pants and rolled my jeans above my knees so I could go into the shallows with him. He was gleeful, frisking about in the water. I was full of love for him, but felt as though I was watching it all through a gauze screen. I looked down at the water swirling around my calves. I couldn't even really tell if it was cold, if I was cold. I was numb.

In the afternoon we went up to the nature reserve at Kennall Vale, with its quarry pits and old waterwheel buildings. It's an exciting place and always makes Matt and me think of Gruffalos and Harry Potter and monsters. Matt foraged for sticks to use as wands and gave me a good one so that I could cast a Patronus in case we met any Dementors. I waved my wand and tried to summon up the necessary happy memories and good feelings but it was a struggle.

On Boxing Day my mum and I went out for a walk around the lanes of Ponsanooth. Up Ghost Hill, past Kennall Vale, across Laity Moor, past the farmhouse where the dog always barks, down Speech Lane and on to Frog Hill. I wanted to see if it was still possible to get close to the viaduct, as Matty and I used to. We'd clamber over the fence and head for the river past Bluebell Island.

We walked further down the hill, treading the route my granny used to take to catch the bus to Truro, where she worked as a typist at a solicitor's firm and then, later, in an old people's home, never dreaming that everyone she looked after would outlive her. She always carried a packet of Polos in her bag and used to give one to a horse that would come ambling across when he saw her. We tried to work out which field that would have been.

We turned around just short of the main road and headed back up.

'So, Ca, what do you think about the ashes?' my mum said. 'Do you want to do something about them this holiday? We don't need to organize the plaque at the same time. We could do that later.'

Every time I thought about it I felt a brick of despair in my tummy and tears jumped into my eyes.

'I don't know,' I said.

'Well, there's no rush.'

It wasn't supposed to be a joke but after a few seconds we both laughed.

'We probably should. I'm scared of it. Scared of how it will make me feel.'

'Maybe it's one of those things where the anticipation is worse.'

We trudged upwards.

'You know, I think we should do it,' I said. 'It's not like it will be any easier in the future.'

'Do you want to see them?'

'Yes. I suppose. I don't know. Maybe we could do it on New Year's Day.'

'Or New Year's Eve, maybe? The last day of the year?'

'Yes, that's a good idea. Let's do that.'

I slept well the night before. My mum told me she'd woken up at five and had been having lots of good thoughts about Matty.

The ashes were under my parents' bed.

'They're bigger and heavier than you'd think,' my mum said, pulling out a large package.

We opened the cardboard box. The brown plastic container inside was about the size and shape of an old-fashioned sweet jar, the type they used to have in the village shop where Matty and I would buy our quarter of pear drops or pineapple cubes. I held it against me.

Maybe I was imagining it, but I felt a warmth from it. I cuddled it to my chest. I'm holding what's left of Matty against my heart, I thought.

It was beautiful, and I felt calmer. There was nothing to be frightened of. I thought of Matty's great height, of all the space he took up when he was alive, and wondered if a littler person would have a smaller pot of ashes.

I put the box in my blue-and-white Musto bag. I didn't want to let go of it but I needed to have a pee before we set off and it felt weird to take Matty with me so I left him on the bed. I remembered being completely freaked out at my granddad's funeral when one of his sisters told me he would always look down on me and I really disliked the thought of him watching me on the toilet or picking my nose.

We got into the car. My parents in the front; me, Matt and Matty on the back seat.

Dad had suggested the place, the cliffs down by Little Dennis where we went swimming one Easter when we were maybe ten and eleven. Dad had said he'd go in the water if we did, so we dived in joyously, telling him it wasn't cold, and he followed to find the water freezing.

We parked at Pendennis Point but couldn't manage to find a path down to the right spot so we drove around the corner, parked further along and found a set of stone steps.

The wind was whipping the sea over the rocks. Mum, Dad and Matt stayed back as I sat on an outcrop of rock and shuffled myself further out. I undid the Sellotape from the neck of the jar. The ashes were browner than I was expecting, more the colour of red granite than grey ash. I looked back at my parents and Matt behind me, down into the sea and up at the sky, and gave the urn a mighty heave.

We watched Matty swirl into the air. The sea was lapping at the rocks. It was exhilarating. Again and again I threw. There were bits of ash on my trainers, on my tracksuit bottoms. I screwed the lid on to the urn and put it back in the bag. I saw a bit of ash on my fingers and rubbed it on my topaz necklace. It felt magical to have liberated Matty to the air and the sea on a beautifully wild and dramatic New Year's Eve.

I felt a physical release. As I stood up, my body felt straighter; the weight across my shoulders had lifted. The world was bright. I could choose to feel Matty wherever I wanted, in the trees or near the sea.

I knew I would remember this as a happy day and wondered if Matt would remember it, too. I clambered back over the rocks and offered him my hand. He took it and together we walked up the stone steps.

'Did you call me Matthew because of your brother, Mummy?'

I hadn't intended to. I've always been wary of that impulse to try to see lost loved ones in new babies, but as soon as the sonographer told us we were having a boy it just felt right.

'Yes, darling. Because he was a lovely dude and I knew you would be, too.'

We got back in the car, drove to the Pandora Inn for lunch and then went home, where we played a card game called Newmarket that Matty and I had loved when we were kids and that Matt loves now. Usually we gamble with matchsticks, but today we added a frisson of excitement and competition by using the last of the festive treats, and there was great hilarity over who won the most Ferrero Rocher and chocolate coins.

There was still the plaque to sort and this turned out to have a mountain of administrative difficulties. How often the bureaucracy of death jostles on alongside the feelings. There was also the question of the wording, which my mother was leaving to me. I developed a severe case of writer's block around it, wanting to find an elegant way of marking the difference between Matty's first sixteen years of full life, and then his post-accident fate worse than death, up until the moment he actually died. I didn't like any of the ways I tried to express it and dithered over it for months.

Finally, I realized I was stalling again, and had fallen into the trap of trying to tell the whole story on a small piece of slate. I've written a book about this, I thought. All the unfairness and injustice has been well covered. I thought how we have to tell our stories, feel the pain and then let it go. It was time for me to put the book of Matty on the shelf and find other stories to live and tell.

It has been a long goodbye. There were a surprising number of decisions to make and it often occurred to me that we couldn't have done this any earlier, because we wouldn't have been able to bear the necessary talking about it. In the end, it took the amount of time it needed to take.

I can't quite believe now that I used to get so drunk I might have forgotten dealing with the ashes, but I don't look back with any shame, only a deep, deep sympathy for that poor girl floundering around in all that pain.

'I know you don't like the word, but it's acceptance, isn't it?' my mum said. 'Don't we just have to accept it?'

And I looked into the future, where I stand by Matty's plaque remembering our old jokes before looking up and out over the deep blue Falmouth sea, and said, 'Yes.'

Matthew Peter Mintern

1974 – 1998

Deeply loved, always missed

Ashes scattered at sea

Fear of Dying

In short, know this: Human lives are brief and trivial. Yesterday a blob of semen; tomorrow embalming fluid, ash.

Marcus Aurelius

I've been reading Marcus Aurelius. He was Roman emperor in the second century AD and wrote a series of meditations and reflections, mainly to keep himself on the straight and narrow. It's such a comfort to find out that almost two thousand years ago the Roman emperor was fretting about pretty much the same stuff as I do now. Of course, he didn't have Twitter to navigate, but I guess being emperor and having your face on all the coins leads to some fairly significant authenticity issues. He largely dealt with his worries – his own form of 'avataritis' – by telling himself how unimportant he was in the grand scheme of things. Life is short and fragile, so get on with making of it what you will, is the gist.

I've never been scared of dying, presumably because for a long time I was only grudgingly alive. This, I think, is the legacy of damage. Josephine Hart, in her novel of that name, suggests that damaged people are dangerous because they know they will survive. I love that novel, and there's a poetic beauty to that idea, but I don't think it's true. Not for me. Damaged people know that it can happen again. That's our biggest problem.

How do you move through life with the grim knowledge that the blade can come down at any moment? It might already have fallen, but you haven't had the phone call yet. I get stuck in this a lot – a sudden panic that the thing I fear most has happened but I haven't yet been notified. I don't worry that I will die, I worry that the people I love will die – possibly in some horrible, drawn-out way – and that I will have to bear witness and be found wanting. I'm too aware of the fates worse than death. It's not good for me, of course, to be in this state of constant vigilance. It means that no matter what the benefits of my current situation, I don't trust that a period of good fortune will last.

I have noticed that as the quality of my life increases, as it feels less of a joyless trudge and more of a pleasurable saunter, as I wake up to the idea that I might be able to find life largely enjoyable, as I feel more and more aware of the beauty and possibility in the world and better able to navigate witnessing the unhappiness of others, my fear for my own safety has increased. I'm more nervous around potential danger, more wary of dark alleys. I suppose that makes perfect sense. Now that I'm having a bit of fun playing the game, I don't want it to stop.

Still, even with this new-found appreciation for life, I'm mainly worried about leaving it because I fear abandoning my son. When I was about fifteen my friend and I watched a film called *Who Will Love My Children* in which the dying mother had to parcel out all of her kids, including the ones who weren't especially appealing, and try to find a new wife for her useless husband.

This is the sort of thing I laugh about in daylight and brood over in the small hours. What if I don't have enough time? I worry. What if I am felled by a bus rather than an illness and haven't prepared a really thorough checklist? What will Matt do then?

During a recent spate of nights, I lay awake, mind whirring, pondering the fate of the world, fearing an apocalypse, thinking about Matt and how to keep him safe, about how he'd get on without me. When he was very tiny, I was scared he would die in the night; as he grew older I feared that I'd lose sight of him for a second and he'd toddle into the road or be snatched.

Now I fret about the hurdles he and his little friends will face growing up; they'll have to cope with everything we did, but also navigate online life. I thought how, if I gave in to all my maternal instincts, I would lock Matt in a room and lie down on the floor next to the door – a sort of human draught excluder, not allowing anything in that might corrupt or harm him. Of course, I know this is insane and that one of the worst things we can do for our children is worry too much about them. This is a legacy of trauma: we spend so much time anticipating a new horror that we destroy the present.

So I started mentally composing advice for him in my sleepless hours, in the event of a tragedy that prevented me from handing it over in real life. I started typing it up the next morning and I gradually saw that, perhaps like my granny sitting by her plot in the cemetery, accepting and planning for my death and acknowledging the fragile nature of all life was better for my anxiety than trying to ignore it. And, as I typed away, I wondered to what extent the world is more hostile than it has ever been or whether it's the way we consume it that makes us think it is. I thought about the challenges faced by my cavewoman ancestor, by mothers through the ages, by women who waved their conscripted sons off to war, by both my grandmothers, and I felt reassured and humbled in thinking of myself among them. Whatever comes, I will face it head on. It doesn't serve Matt if my fear for his future well-being prevents me from being a loving and fun mother in the present.

Over time, I grasped that while I couldn't save either Matt or myself from the pain of life, I could share what I'd learned and would probably do well to follow some of my own advice.

Dear Matt,

At the moment you are seven, but I have always thought of you as a grown-up in the making and it's not much of a stretch to imagine the conversations we might have over the years. Hopefully we will get to have them for real, but in case we don't, I am writing a few things down. You can and should of course ignore all of this, but it has amused me to make this list for you.

Most of this is for when you are older. A lot of growing up is about learning to hide how you are feeling so you can protect yourself, and then a lot about being really grown-up is unpicking all those defensive measures and working out who you actually want to be. But for now . . .

Kids can be vile

The absolute two best things about growing up are that people get progressively nicer and you have more control over who you spend time with. Hopefully you have loads of good mates right now but if you don't or if you have to endure unpleasant people at school, I promise you it gets better with age. And always remember . . .

Mean people are sad on the inside

This is the truest thing. People bully from a place of their own pain. When anyone behaves in a way you don't like, it can help to remember that they are probably unhappy and might not even understand it themselves.

Try not to take things personally

When people are horrid or rude, they are probably not trying to be. Assume they are having a bad day/

week/year and try not to get hooked in. I like what my friend Gerard's mum says when faced with strange behaviour: 'God love them, maybe they're not well.'

Be kind rather than clever

There will often be a chance to say or do something unkind, funny or cutting at someone else's expense. It's better to bypass the thrill of showing how clever you are and just be decent instead.

Everything is always less about you than you think it is, and more about you than you think it is

This is a major secret of life. Everything is less about you than you think it is because you are a human being and everything you feel has been felt by others before. Everything is more about you than you think it is because you almost always have more power to affect your circumstances than you think you do.

Do not assume responsibility for the world's problems

Care about other people, but not at the expense of yourself. You come first.

You be you, let everyone else be them

Try not to be critical and judgemental. It never leads to a good place. (This is really hard to do, by the way, but I've worked out that when I get judgemental it's usually more about me than the other person.) Which brings us to:

The 'grown-up on a scooter' rule

When I see a grown-up riding a scooter, sometimes I think, Oooh, what a brilliant thing to do, how lovely, I wish I could do that, maybe I can; and sometimes I have a dark and angry response that contains far too many rude words to write down. This is, of course, more about me than the grown-up on the scooter and I've learned to apply this bit of self-knowledge to stop me raining on the parades of other people and stamping all over things that don't suit my mood. When you feel angry at someone or something, it is really worth considering whether it might be more about you.

Try to paddle your own canoe and not worry about what other people are doing

Comparison, competition and envy are the three evils. It's human to feel them, but it's far better to focus on your own actions. Worry less about the things you can't do and enjoy the things you can. And don't be a nose-turner-upper. You don't have to like everything, but put your energies into seeking out what you love, rather than explaining to everyone else why what they love isn't worth it.

Give everyone the benefit of the doubt as much as you can

Don't make assumptions about what other people may be coping with. You never know the size of someone else's paper round and it's safest to assume that everyone has a cross to bear.

Be curious

Curiosity is a wonderful quality and you don't have to understand everything or have all the answers to enjoy exploring life and ideas.

It's almost always cock-up rather than conspiracy

This is true, especially at work, and it will save you lots of time and stress if you realize other people are usually flawed and careless rather than ill-intentioned.

Want the best for everyone, including yourself

Don't try to make people do what they don't want to do, either by force or by manipulation. It never works out well for anyone in the end.

Try not to be the sort of person who says, 'I'm the sort of person who . . .'

Flexibility is well worth cultivating. Often fear sits behind what we think we dislike and staying open to what life has to offer always reaps rewards.

Make friends with rejection

Who knows how you will decide to earn your money, but learning to cope with rejection is essential for anything where you are aiming high, because there will be a lot of it. This is what I tell unpublished writers and it works for anything that involves exposing yourself to the judgement of others: make it your aim to accumulate rejection letters. Run around the car park with your football rattle waving it in the air. 'Hurray!' you need to shout. 'I did it. I was on the pitch. I tried it. I put myself up for it.' That's the celebration.

Be as honest as you can

No situation is ever improved by secrecy.

Heartbreak and heartache are part of being human

Whether I'm alive or dead, I can't save you from pain. The world can feel like a cruel place sometimes but allow yourself to feel your feelings, ask for help, notice kindness and look for the currants in the cake.

Life is a jigsaw puzzle

Sometimes you might feel as though you're losing your pieces or they don't fit. Try not to worry too much about this. Focus on putting together the parts you can do. We are inclined to be angry with ourselves for not having everything sorted, but there's so much to see, to feel and to learn. Not only is perfection impossible, but wouldn't it actually be really dull?

As Oscar Wilde said, 'We are all in the gutter, but some of us are looking at the stars'

Life is hard for everyone, at least some of the time. Whenever I am weighed down by the grind of life, it helps me to take a few deep breaths and look for the stars.

Do your best. Be kind and helpful

I've pinched that from the Beavers. It's a pretty good aim. Sometimes you might not feel you are capable of doing your best, and that's fine too. There are days when it is enough just to aim to not make your own or anyone else's life any worse.

Don't worry about not being happy

Life isn't supposed to be a non-stop ego-stroking

barrage of treats. Trying to be happy has never worked for me. If I lower my expectations about what I'm entitled to, if I try to be useful, if I look for ways to create meaning and purpose for myself and others, then something akin to happiness shimmers into view.

Love is the answer and the antidote

I do so hope that we get to spend a lot of time together but, whatever happens, I hope you will always know you were deeply, deeply loved. It might not have seemed that way when I was shouting at you about getting your socks on or finishing your porridge, but I was always full of love for you. Love widely, love often, I'd say. Love with your whole heart even as you fear it wouldn't survive the loss. Anything else is not being fully alive.

You will make mistakes

Of course you will. Making mistakes is how we learn.

It's OK to change your mind

I used to have lots of opinions and the older I get the less convinced I am of anything. The only thing I know for sure is that more connects us than divides us and there is always a need for more kindness and tolerance in the world.

YOYOB – You Own Your Own Behaviour

This is very true. As Viktor Frankl says, 'Everything can be taken from a man but one thing: the last of the human freedoms – to choose one's attitude in any given set of circumstances, to choose one's own way.'

Try to be a decent human, put more good than bad into the world, but always put yourself first and accept that it is OK to be flawed. If you can treat yourself with love and respect then all good things will follow. Remember, you are special, and so is everybody else.

Ignore all my advice

You should of course ignore all this if you want to,

as you often ignore the very good advice I give you now. (I haven't included here the nugget of wisdom that it is better to get jobs and homework done straight away, as I share that with you on a near daily basis at the moment and you show no inclination to ever agree with me.)

I want to sign off by telling you to be safe. That's my job as your mother, my evolutionary purpose: to try to keep you safe.

But I won't. I'm remembering us chasing Dementors in Kennall Vale. I kept the wand you gave me that day. I washed it under the outside tap and carried it up from Cornwall to London, where it sits on my desk, reminding me of you and me and magic. I'm picking it up now and I'm casting you a spell with which I endow you with resilience, curiosity, kindness, a healthy ability to take risks and, of course, love.

I am your mother and you are my son, and this will

always be so. The time I had with you was a privilege and an honour.

Live, love, jump, my darling boy.

A Deathbed Perspective

One of my favourite novels is *Moon Tiger* by Penelope Lively. The heroine, Claudia Hampton, is a writer who has lived a long, eventful life studded with both success and sorrow. Now, as she lies dying in her hospital bed, drifting in and out of consciousness, Claudia remembers her life in all its intensity, all her loves, triumphs, disappointments and heartaches. I've been recommending this novel for years – I like short books about unconventional women, about love, about the Second World War and about the nature of history and storytelling – but I've only recently realized exactly why I love it so much, what urges me to press it on to friends. It's because it offers hope and an ambition of sorts.

Claudia navigates the pain of life sufficiently to stick with it, to carry on playing the game, to attain her deathbed perspective.

This is what I aspire to, for myself and the people I love and everyone in the world: that we manage to weather the storms of life and achieve the long view. I want us to be able to look back at joy and grief at the end of a long life, and see the way they wove together.

Lately I've been finding it helpful to inject this perspective into my day. When I can't decide whether or not to do something, I ask myself what I will wish I'd done at the end of my long life. When I feel cross or sad about something, I ask myself whether I'll still care about it on my deathbed.

I find this an extremely calming and helpful way to think, a good way of working out what is important. I know that when I'm dying I won't wish I'd spent more time nursing a hangover or on Twitter getting wound up about other people's opinions. I won't wish I'd owned more stuff or lived in a bigger house. I will be glad I worked hard, I will be glad if I was in any way useful or made a difference. I will never think that an act of kindness was a waste of time. I will be pleased I wrote some books – hopefully lots – and I know I'll be grateful for every bit of love and every single joke. I'll think of all my significant people, of the way we were with each other, and I'll remember the kindness of strangers, the joy of my friends and my good fortune in being born into a beautiful family.

Years ago I read a novel called *The Colour of Heaven* by James Runcie in which one character asks another whose voice they would want to hear when they were dying. It stopped me in my tracks. I was in one of those tatty relationships at the time, in which none of our attraction to each other had ever managed to translate into a good kind of love. I wouldn't want to hear *his* voice when I was dying, I thought, or, even if I did, he wouldn't be there, he'd be off somewhere else, up to no good, trying to chat up one of my friends.

I was lonely at the time, mourning my dead brother

and adrift in a sea of misery, unable to see the other side. I couldn't imagine that I would ever find anyone to love me, that I would ever have a child, that I would find a living voice I wanted to hear. Now I think I will hear a cacophony. I'm not going to settle for one voice: I want a choir of all the people I've ever loved to sing me to my last sleep. I imagine a beautiful, possibly morphine-induced vision of the living and the dead singing their hearts out and smiling at me right up until the moment I close my eyes.

I've made friends with both life and death. I've realized it is a sacred duty to be with someone when they are dying and I'm finally glad I had the privilege of helping my brother through his long death. I'm honoured to have stood shoulder to shoulder with my friends as they have coped with all kinds of loss. If things follow their natural order, I will carry out that duty for my parents. I know now that there will be a sweetness to the grief I'll feel for them, as I know that's what they want. They want me to outlive them. They'd like to be able to die at the same time as each other, knowing that Matt and I are safe. They already feel they've achieved something in the longevity stakes, as they have both lived longer than any of their parents did. My mother told me recently that she wakes up every morning thinking, Oooh, I'm still alive. I've got another day. That seems like an excellent attitude to cultivate.

If we think in terms of content and process, then life itself is the process, a journey from innocence to experience. Let's hope we'll all look back on our content from our deathbeds, probably still with sadness, but also with joy.

It is, we know, better to have loved and lost than never to have loved at all. The big question is, once you've experienced the grenade, once the guillotine has fallen, how do you live with the knowledge that it can happen again? We all want self-protection, emotional body armour, yet the only way to protect against loss is to avoid love at all costs. And that is no way to live.

So, how do we live and love even as we know that everything might change in an instant? This is what I think I know now. We don't need to fix our broken hearts so much as realize that they never stop growing. We have an infinite capacity for love. Once we accept that heartache is part of being human, we can acknowledge our pain, feel our feelings and stop running away. Then we can look for ways to be of service, enjoy the currants in the cake and think, What a thing it is to be alive in this beautiful world.

Inspiring Addendum

These days, almost nothing thrills me more than finding out the granular details of other people's lives, regimes, and coping strategies. It makes me feel less alone and gives me inspiration. I find it both comforting and stimulating to map myself against other humans; I like getting tips but I equally enjoy thinking, Well, I'd never want to do that. So I asked some writers I admire to share how they hold steady and what they do to feel better. The result is a beautiful collage of philosophical approaches and practical suggestions that perfectly underlines how humans are both the same and different, and that there are few blanket rules, but lots of possibilities.

* * *

As a sober alcoholic who has dealt with serious depression and my share of tragedy, I have some time-tested things I do to feel better. They're simple and maybe corny and entirely unoriginal and they often work.

The first thing I do is I accept how I feel, be it sad, angry or afraid. Then, since I'm forty-five and not twenty-five, I remember all of the things and feelings that have risen up, come to a boil and then passed on through me over the years. Good and bad. They all pass. 'Middle' age has some benefits and one of them is that a good pile of years offers anyone proof that nothing lasts forever, including a bad feeling, no matter what causes it.

I can do that part sitting still.

Then I get up and go for a run or a swim if circumstances allow. The run can be a walk if I don't have running clothes and the swim can be a cold shower or bath (the cold is important) if there's no other water nearby.

Then I set a timer for twenty-five minutes and tidy and/or do whatever other horrific task I've been avoiding. Washing up, replying to messages, taking out the rubbish, whatever. It just matters that I do it at a good clip and don't stop until the timer is up.

After I do the exercise and the twenty-five minutes of horror, I might just treat myself to a hand job.

Rob Delaney, author of *A Heart That Works*

If advising someone else, I'd say do something intensely physical like swimming or cycling if possible, or prune a shrub and do some sweeping, even just clean the bathroom properly, including the drains (with soda crystals, distilled vinegar, boiling water). Then cook yourself a lentil soup from scratch. This fills your home with the comforting aroma of toasted spices. Once that's done, let it sit while you have a bath or shower. After dinner, have an early night, you'll be tired. Listen to a soothing audiobook, say, Wodehouse read by Martin Jarvis or *Winnie the Pooh* by Stephen Fry. Fall asleep.

Alternatively, phone someone who likes you. Get them to compare you favourably to cousins who haven't done quite as well as you (in spite of public school) or they have, but aren't as nice.

Nina Stibbe, author of *Love, Nina*

I grew up convinced that nothing could ever happen to me that hadn't already been experienced by someone in a novel somewhere. I'm aware that sounds like magical thinking, but as a result I have always seen novels as a blueprint for getting through difficult experiences. No matter what I've been worried about – death, bereavement, heartbreak, war, politicians – novels have helped me to pin the worry down and put it into perspective. But then I wrote one, and I realized that this aspect of reading fiction had been 'ruined' for me. I am hoping it's temporary. While I wait, I'm filling the gap with non-fiction, including podcasts and documentaries. Something about sinking myself into a narrative usually pulls me out of my own troubles in a way I find cathartic.

Sara Collins, author of
The Confessions of Frannie Langton

When things go badly wrong, I come off social media. I tell my husband that I'm fine. I cuddle the dog. I go for a walk. I tell my husband that I'm actually not fine and he gives me some sensible advice, which I ignore. I play the piano and the dog wanders off to another room. I lie in bed for half an hour. I take my husband's advice.

Adam Kay, author of *This is Going to Hurt*

The first thing I do is get outside, ideally in nature. I walk or run or cycle, move my body. Whatever the weather. However awful I feel, I feel better if I go outside and move. If I am really troubled I will go for a walk with a family member or a friend, walking and talking is unbelievably good therapy, followed by a treat – mine is a cuppa tea and cake. Another thing I do is get tidying; it doesn't really sort my ruminating mind but I do find it comforting and it brings order in that tiny domain when the rest of the world is chaotic. My attitude is I need to face and come to terms with whatever is troubling me. Sometimes I can find ways to repair or even fix it, but often I have to come to terms with it, allow the feelings of distress to come through my body (which walking helps with), name it (talking to someone) and then intentionally do things that comfort me (cuppa).

Julia Samuel, author of *Grief Works*

If I want to feel better, I listen to *Leonard Cohen Live in London (2009)*, on a continual loop. Always does the trick.

Philippe Sands, author of *East West Street*

Depends on how wrong. If we're talking 5/10 – in other words, if I know there's hope or deep down I know the answer – I have a little cry and a lot of biscuits, I have an online shop and a lot of daytime telly. I unplug from whatever I've done or has been done to me and don't dwell until the dwelling brings relief and a way out.

If we're talking 10/10 wrong then I retreat to my family, my children, very few friends. I go where I know people have my back, where I can collapse and not speak, where I don't have to make sense, where I can swear, rail against the world, repeat myself, not sleep. I go, physically as well as emotionally, where I'll find succour and strength and sometimes a telling off but mostly not, where there's history and knowingness, unchangeable things, where love lives.

Kit de Waal, author of
Without Warning and Only Sometimes

I always expect things to go wrong. I'm not surprised if the roof leaks just after it was supposedly fixed or when someone dies. We're all going to die and knowing that helps me make the best of people when they and I are still alive. As for trying to feel better, it depends on why I'm not feeling okay to start with. Sometimes I stay with not being better. It takes patience.

Phillipa Perry, author of
The Book You Wish Your Parents Had Read

Since I was a small child I've been instinctively drawn to the one thing that stops the ground shaking beneath my feet. Without quite knowing why – in those times when I feel like an apple about to fall from a tree, when it's a long way down and there's no way back – I always find myself running to the fields and the woods. Something about breathing in the deep green air of the forest, or the salt of the coast, brings life right back down into the moment. Feeling the wind on my skin, zipping my coat against the rain – the elemental contact has an immediacy that stops the earth vibrating and allows a sense of stillness to return. That and a lot of hot tea!

Raynor Winn, author of *The Salt Path*

I lie in bed with one of my children (either will do) after they have fallen asleep and I read a book. Sometimes I take a tiny hand and place it on my own heartbeat. Being close to my child and burying my nose in a book have always been the two things that ground me in my own body, better than anything else I've found. To do both at once gives me the best possible shot at making my way back to base camp.

Pandora Sykes, author of *What Writers Read*

I ask myself if it is not, in fact, alright to feel sad. We are urged to hurry on from sadness like it is something embarrassing, when in fact we are allowed to feel it and not only on those occasions sanctified, such as the loss of a loved one. The question for me is, is this passing sadness or is this deep trauma – an echo of a past awfulness that some event in the Now has attuned me to back in the Then? I've learned that trauma makes itself known but doesn't always announce itself – the 'work' of being an adult has been, for me, learning to recognize it. To feel that tension behind my eyes and realise it's not because I've been reading too much.

Sadness in the Now is not the same as sadness, or badness, in the Then (trauma). They are different problems and ask for different solutions. To feel better in the Now, I might reread a book or poem I know I will enjoy – Mary Oliver is never not comforting, especially her audiobooks. I wish I could go for a walk with Mary on the beach in Provincetown. Also in the Now, I might take myself out for a walk and while I am there – and depending how bad things are – shout into the wind and let it carry my feelings away. This is especially good on a cold winter's day up on the South Downs.

If what I am dealing with is trauma – that's to say, something in the present has sent me off on an unhappy wander into the past . . . then I try to be compassionate to that past self, to that wee boy. I might give him the things he didn't have Then – a warm blanket, a quiet room, a friend he can talk to safely. Therapy helps. Increasingly I find doing something for others lifts me out of myself – whether that is activism or just the giving of attention. Wherever, or whenever, my sadness is coming from, I find that cuddling a chicken makes me happy.

Damian Barr, author of *Maggie and Me*

Walk to the nearest park and watch dogs running about. Dogs in parks always find reasons to run, even if no one is chasing them or throwing a ball for them; it's impossible not to think that they're running for the sheer joy of it. It always lifts the spirits. (So perhaps the real answer is, seek out something that radiates joy.)

Kamila Shamsie, author of *Best of Friends*

I have generalized anxiety disorder. This means that a bit of my brain is in a constant state of training, waiting and disaster preparedness. I am in the Marines of things going wrong. But being in the throes of disaster itself is nowhere near as awful as planning, predicting and imagining it. The hard thing – but potentially the life and sanity saving thing – is to keep that knowledge close. We think we can't deal with the disaster itself. What we are struggling with is what we anxiously predict the disaster may become.

My favourite Instagram account, Poster Journal, has

a meme I love. It's a picture of a bright yellow sun, with the caption 'Nothing is forever you silly bitch'. When things go wrong, we become terribly frightened of coping with forever. We only ever have to cope with a minute, an hour or maybe a day at a time. It is possible to make those minutes into beautiful beads and start stringing them together. That's when we start to understand how strong we are.

We think we must panic and try to resolve the problem by relentlessly pushing onwards and upwards. But if we rest, and find brief solace in a book or a bath, solutions often surprise us from the side. Give yourself whatever you need, moment by moment, to bring yourself comfort. Sometimes, any activity seems impossible but I have never, ever regretted taking a fifteen-minute break and going for a walk.

Daisy Buchanan, author of *Careering*

Whenever I'm truly lost or absolutely stuck, I write a letter from my much older self to the me of here, now. It's a way of summoning a wiser, kinder perspective – a tangible one, too. Something to hold close, for courage.

Tanya Shadrick, author of *The Cure for Sleep*

Only one thing works completely reliably for me, and that is to find the constructive action I'm willing to take. Imagine a Venn diagram consisting of two circles: at any moment, there's a huge set of things that 'need doing', and another set of things I'm actually willing to do. On my bad days, most of that second circle is filled with things like 'listlessly scroll through social media', 'feel sorry for myself', 'eat comfort food I don't even really enjoy' or 'snap at other people'. But if I can remember to stop, and get quiet and listen to myself in a spirit of friendliness, I'll find that there's somewhere those two circles overlap: there's always something constructive I'm willing to do. Maybe it's nothing more than loading the dishwasher, or sweeping the floor, or cleaning up my computer desktop, or going for a five-minute walk. Fine. It doesn't matter how small it is. The point (though I'm still liable to forget it) is that constructive action is incompatible with total despair. Once you're making any positive difference – even just to the state of the kitchen floor – feeling at least a little bit better seems like an automatic consequence.

Oliver Burkeman, author of *Four Thousand Weeks*

When I wobble, when I feel an unravelling lurking, I take it to the water. I swim outside, and every time I do this it resets my dial back to normal, or whatever is normal for me. The darkness dissolves and the light is let in. Something about the sounds around me being altered as I swim, something about how it slows everything down, something about the sharpness of the cold and the sense of an unexpected adventure lifts my spirit. No two swims are the same, nature is unpredictable that way. Each experience is different and this helps you deal with change, life is constant change and in the water that sense of change is reinforced, being able to cope there means I can cope everywhere. I like to swim at sunrise, or as close to it as possible, so a hopeful change hangs in the air, a new day of possibility. And of course, the swimming women beside the lakes, the lidos, the seas, radiate positivity (and cake, there is a lot of cake). You cannot be in a bad mood around the outdoor swimming women, for what we do is frankly ridiculous, especially in winter, and we recognize that about each other, it's our bond. So search for your swimming, it's probably outside because nature is the best place to find the ups in the middle of the downs. And find your people, if we want to feel better it is our connection to others that will nourish us most.

Lorraine Candy, author of
Mum, What's Wrong with You?

The most important thing I've learned re wellbeing is just this: DO IT. Whatever makes you feel better, even briefly, do it. Cancel plans. Ask for support. Be upfront about your needs. Go to the GP. Take meds if you need them.

For a long time, I thought if I was open about my needs I would suffer stigma. Quite the opposite. Being open about the scaffolding I sometimes need to do my job means my colleagues can make contingencies before we even start. I used to think that getting help was cheating somehow, that I should tough it out alone. No more. Again, just do it.

This comes with a caveat, obviously. Sometimes coping strategies can seem helpful (note how I refrain from calling them good or bad) when, in fact, they aren't. I still have to work on identifying when my instincts are actually my anxieties trying to shrink my life down to nothing. It's about finding ways I can make my life a little bit easier but still exploit all the opportunities that come my way.

You don't get a prize for struggling through life. It's not Tough Mudder. Take the easiest route, cheat, cut corners.

Juno Dawson, author of *Her Majesty's Royal Coven*

I swear and cry at the past and the future. Then I make space between them to find small moments, filling them with sights, sounds and the companionship of the wild, especially birds. The wild helps me feel alive, while offering perspective and showing resilience. Most importantly, it gives me the gift of the present. (If I need a hug, I've always turned to my dog first.)

Hannah Bourne-Taylor, author of *Fledgling*

When things seem bleak, I try to force myself to remember that this too shall pass. It is not always easy, so, yes, I do allow myself to wallow and mope. I think pretending that everything is OK or believing that I am pathetic for feeling sad is unhealthy. Sadness is a valid and valuable emotion too, and it should be given its rightful place. But, much like joy, pain is also ephemeral, and sunlight will always find its way through the cracks. I have a picture on my phone that I once took of a tiny purple flower popping its head out of a cracked concrete pavement, and it always makes me smile. There will always be moments of beauty when life feels completely desolate. Through these fallow periods, I also try to sketch, paint, draw, make linocut prints. I sometimes write stories and rubbish poems, knowing full well that fiction and poetry are not my forte. I find that creativity, especially if I do not attach external validation to it, is very meditative. It always makes me happy. It always reminds me of the beauty around me, and that I am capable of producing. And then there are my children. They are the most beautiful people, and even in all the pain and agony of motherhood, they are a constant reminder of the joy and hope in this world. They are my anchor and my northern star.

Pragya Agarwal, author of *Hysterical*

Solvitur ambulando – it is solved by walking – may be as close to a personal mantra as I can muster. If things are a little much or I am in search of clarity or positivity, putting one foot in front of the other is the shortest cut to that place. Walking gives my brain just enough to do to stop it searching for something to attach to; an empty peace descends, and like a sock full of marbles, I find I – and anything that might be troubling me – shake down into a better order. Intuitive leaps are made, ideas hatch without effort or engagement; I stop thinking and somehow become more creative.

Mark Diacono, author of *Spice: A Cook's Companion*

My answer to how to feel better is included in the question because the answer is 'to feel'. Like so many of us, as a kid I was trained not to express difficult feelings and wasn't 'held and heard' when tough stuff happened. This meant that my feelings became split off in separate parts of myself, except at times when life became overwhelming. At those times I was flooded with unbearably intense emotions for years until I could get the lid back on.

An understanding of trauma and plurality is helping me to befriend those lost parts of me, to bring them home and to finally feel the feelings they've carried for so long: the terror, rage, shame and grief.

I'd recommend any practice that can help you to slowly, gently allow your feelings and welcome them with kindness. I find focusing and meditation practices helpful where you try to experience or describe the quality or energy of the feeling rather than being caught up in all the swirling thoughts around it. I'm also finding it useful to draw the feelings as monsters, to journal about them and to talk through my experiences with a trauma-sensitive therapist.

Meg-John Barker, author of *Rewriting the Rules*

I plant my feet firmly and I slow my breathing, breathing in deep from the diaphragm. I close my eyes for at least ten seconds. I visualize drawing energy from the ground into my feet. And I tell myself really firmly that I've got this. Also I laugh . . . a lot.

Lucy Easthope, author of *When the Dust Settles*

I have a number of things I do, all of them only temporary fixes, but they do work in the short term. Music is restorative, especially music that makes me move, although anything I find beautiful is helpful. Sometimes a repeating loop is necessary. This has the added advantage of taking me away from the current political news, which otherwise I follow to my doom.

Or I might look for videos online of dogs being adopted or reunited with loved ones. Cat videos are also good. Somewhere out there a lab chimp is feeling grass under its feet for the first time. The necessary storyline is one of rescue.

Or I might start a new Korean drama, something like *Our Blues* or *My Mister*. These shows often run around sixteen episodes so they provide several hours of concentrated diversion.

Books are the best, of course. In times of trouble, I go to books I've already read. Rereading is an underappreciated activity. You always find things you didn't see before or perhaps saw, but didn't remember, and you don't risk the disappointment of a book you won't like.

Karen Joy Fowler, author of
We Are All Completely Beside Ourselves

When things are bad my cure-all is to get outside, away from phones and computers. Either I'll work in the garden or greenhouse, where there is always tidying up or planting to be done, or I'll walk across the fields to the sea with the dogs. In fact, I find spending time with a dog or two cures most ills; they are very easily pleased and come with no trite solutions or salt-in-the-wound questioning.

Patrick Gale, author of Mother's Boy

In order to feel better, it's important for me to first determine whether I need alone time, or I need company. This is crucial – because often different sadnesses need different medicines. If I need company, I call a friend, or my sister, or make a dinner arrangement with my husband, preferably involving cheese or pasta. If I need alone time,

I usually get my weighted blanket out. I might put on something soothing like an old film or a programme with David Attenborough's voice. I may read a book about cooking (two favourites: *In the Kitchen: Essays on Food and Life* and *An Everlasting Meal* by Tamar Adler). I may make a big bowl of cacio e pepe. Or borrow a friend's dog. Or go for a long walk in a big coat and call a friend or listen to a chatty podcast (like *Fortunately*). One of these options never fails to make me feel a bit better. They're like old classic songs on an album – they never fail to lift my spirits enough to try again tomorrow.

Emma Gannon, author of *Disconnected*

One thing that has made a difference to me in the last few years when things have gone wrong is to make sure that I say so. The act of stating, either to those around me or simply to myself, 'Things are really shit right now,' is not giving up or giving in. It's being honest. And honesty is a powerful thing.

Marianne Levy, author of *Don't Forget to Scream*

The route to feeling better is a road with two forks. Down one road lie the things we know we shouldn't use to make us feel better but we use them anyway because we know that they do make us feel better, temporarily. (But they really do work, unfortunately, which is why this is a road well travelled for me). This road features these kinds of options: eating three slices of homemade cake wedged together, mainlining two blood orange margaritas in a row (and I really mean in a row), feasting on the one-star reviews of the books of people we don't like. That kind of thing. Don't pretend you don't know what I'm talking about. This road is one big old pity party and you know it's a wrong turning. But sometimes you've got to take the wrong way before you can get back on track. I don't mean to be flippant about this road, though. A lot of the things we do in order to feel better in the short term cause appalling damage in the long term. If overeating turns into not looking after yourself, if over-drinking turns into an alcohol issue and if reading other people's reviews makes you into a comparison-obsessed narcissistic monster . . . then you've turned an occasional unpleasant habit into an intractable issue. The trick is to allow yourself to be human from time to time (i.e. a terrible person). But don't turn that into your entire way of life.

Down the other road lie the things we know are healthier ways of making us feel better. These things are long-term, sensible and fulfilling. They are also quite boring and annoying. Definitions include going for a walk or a swim; working for twenty minutes, taking a break for five minutes and then working again; sacking the day off because you have realized that you are actually falling asleep; calling a trusted old friend; observing routines and rituals that mean nothing to anyone apart from you; listening to the same song on repeat very loudly, ideally singing along ('Honesty' by Billy Joel currently occupies this role for me). Watching stupid cat videos falls somewhere between these two paths. Sometimes it's productive, relaxing and rewarding. Other times you know you're just wasting time on purpose to torture your future regretful self. The key is to try and incorporate the sensible things as often as you can so that you don't feel bad about taking the odd inevitable wrong turn.

The thing is, I don't think we are always meant to 'feel better'. Often, we feel bad for very good reasons and it will take us a while to work them through. Feeling bad is underrated. If you can work out exactly why you feel bad and what that means, that can be incredibly useful in life. Sometimes that is more useful than finding a way – whether that route is sensible or drenched in tequila – to make yourself feel better. In short: don't feel bad about feeling bad. And don't feel bad about the things that make you feel better. Unless they really are ruining your life. Oh, I nearly forgot the one thing that has always made me feel better (although sometimes it makes me feel worse first): therapy.

Viv Groskop, author of *How to Own the Room*

I'm not proud of this, but to feel better I tend to run through my regularly updated mental checklist of all the people who are doing even worse than me. Then I can congratulate myself for not being bottom of the class, take a breath and get back on with it. When things go very wrong, I survive one hour at a time until the end of the day. Get some sleep. Start again. I did it for three months in 2020 when looking after a teenager who was too ill to keep themself alive. We're both still here. I genuinely see this as my greatest achievement.

Michael Brooks, author of *The Maths That Made Us*

Good advice is always hard to take on board in the middle of a crisis. And very often the most well-intended advice arrives at the precise time it is hardest to absorb. The one thing that I get stuck with is the idea, well, of being stuck. What I try and tell myself is to remember that there would be no crisis in the first place if things didn't change, and that change is the one constant in life. So whatever changed to make you feel bad can change again. Even if the change is simply a change in perspective. As the Stoics realized two whole millennia before cognitive behavioural therapy was invented, the ultimate power we have isn't the power over events, but over our reaction to them. So rather than always wanting in a futile way for the world to be just so, we can work on our reactions to change, our acceptance of it, and our faith that where change exists, so does hope.

Neuroplasticity, the concept that our brains literally change their molecular structure, through experience and what we learn, testifies to this. We become slightly different people through our lives. So if we feel we aren't built for something, or aren't made to handle something, it is a comfort to know that we aren't a fixed thing. We could – and will – become someone different, someone possibly stronger, further along life's road. So in a way change can become, paradoxically, the constant we turn to for comfort.

Matt Haig, author of *The Midnight Library*

When things feel difficult and the days seem to blur, I look for joy in the small things. A hot shower, a long walk while looking up at the sky, tea in a porcelain cup. I write lists of all the things I'm grateful for with a fountain pen on thick paper. I'll go to the cinema alone or sit at a cafe with a notebook and daydream. I wait for the moment when I can feel my heartbeat and the breath in my body, until I find an awareness, when I can remind myself of being in a moment, of being alive.

Catherine Cho, author of *Inferno*

I started humming when I lived in Canada and was walking in the forest to try to relieve my back pain. I was a city girl, terrified of silence and being alone, and I hummed because I had been told that it was good to make noise, to let the bears know you were nearby. But I discovered that it also kept me company, with the added benefit of helping to ease my pain. It was a combination of taking my attention from the pain and focusing on the vibration of the hum – moving breath through the body instead of holding it tight and connecting me with myself. Try it. A gentle hum. Starting short and then letting it roam. You can hum with the world around you. The sound of the traffic, the birds, the sound of trees rustling. If you feel like it, after a while, open your mouth. Let the hum out. You might be surprised by what emerges. I wrote a whole album of songs this way.

I often say to people who don't think they can sing: singing is just humming with your mouth open. It is impossible to hum and continue feeling stuck. It always moves you on.

Kate Dimbleby, author of *Sing Happy*

I am very much of the belief that when all is awful you have to find something sweet to remind you, this too shall pass. It can't be cheap sweetness, sugar itself is not the balm; for me, the cure-all is cake. Homemade by yourself or (if that is too much) made by someone else. But love must be one of its ingredients, made by someone who took time to measure it all out exactly, whisk it till it was just right, hold the sieve up high so it would be a little lighter. It needn't be pretty or perfect, but it must have slowed someone else's day, as they took a moment to make a buttery-sweet or chocolatey-squidge sponge-full-of-joy that is now yours – for a brief moment.

And when you eat it, you are reminded that you are not alone, that other people out there like good cake as much as you do. That reminder that cake exists, is often all I need to pull me from the fog, and when I'm very much buried in the mists, I make one myself. To methodically follow someone else's advice, to do as they say and as they did and end up with warmth in cake form is a connecting experience. It doesn't solve everything, but most days it's enough to remind you that sadness can come and go, just as the slice will eventually be finished, but you can always make more cake – or happiness.

Cariad Lloyd, author of *You Are Not Alone*

I'd like to tell you that I find serenity easy these days, but that simply isn't true. When things happen that threaten the wellbeing or happiness of people I love, I find my mind in a turmoil of catastrophic thoughts that tense up my body. It's exhausting! I find peace by coming out of my mind and all that unhelpful 'what if'-ing to focus on being here: right here, right now.

That might mean walking out of doors, to watch nature and focus on its long, enduring timescales that dwarf the temporary weather of our human difficulties; or sitting on our swing with a cup of tea, being aware of the warm cup, the soothing taste, the gentle movement of the seat, the noise of bees in the meadow around me – and usually there's an inquisitive hen requesting attention. Getting lost in an activity helps: I once crawled around the grass to count the tiny, new leaves of spotted orchids that were just emerging while I waited for news about a frightening health scare. Nights are the worst time when we are deeply troubled, aren't they? I've learned to focus on my breath, to mentally trace the shape of my body against the mattress, savour the cool patches of the bed, and relax with each out-breath, deeper and deeper. Most of all, it helps to be kind to ourselves. Mantras like 'I'm doing my best' and 'It won't always feel like this' can really help to refocus from the frenzy to a gentler place where there is still room for peace, even joy, despite the difficulties.

Kathryn Mannix, author of *With the End in Mind*

Being a person of faith helps – I tell myself there must be a wisdom behind disaster, but I just can't see it yet. Still, when the anxiety sets in, it's useful to remind myself that nothing stays the same forever. Everything changes, and so, too, will this. If that fails, then sleep.

Ayisha Malik, author of *The Movement*

I've never felt as represented in fiction as I did, recently, coming to this line in *Unless* by Carol Shields: 'Ms. Winters of Orangetown much prefers the more calculated protocols of dodging sadness with her deliberate manoeuvres.' Because Ms. Winters [not my real name] of [redacted] is naturally inclined to sadness, and while I've come to accept that as my wiring, I refuse to accept it as a daily state. And there, I've learned that the energy it takes to feel better is better spent in advance, on not letting myself feel bad in the first place.

I hope it doesn't sound flippant, I really mean it – I depend absolutely on protocols and deliberate manoeuvres to keep level. Getting up early, always making the bed, dressing as though I don't work from home even though I do, being thoughtful about eating (not over- or under- or distractedly), remembering that television is lovely for intentional watching at night, and depressing AF to just have on all day, a dog walk, better two walks (with two dogs), things like that, and they're just my ones – I'm sure there are lots of people who find background television and the freedom not to make the bed to be good preventions. They're also small, so it's odd that sometimes I wish I could skip them and still feel fine, but I can't. So I make myself, knowing that

– although small – they stack up and save me the more exhausting work of falling into and climbing out of troughs.

What they stack up to, I realize now, is a sense of containment and safety. If polyvagal theory is to be believed (and by me, it so is – I hope you'll Google it) then safety is our fundamental and foremost need and we can't feel loved, attached, happy or energized if we don't feel safe, first. So, I suppose what Ms Winters [name changed to protect identity] really prefers, and has learned to practise, are security measures against the small assaults of the everyday. Duvet-straightening and dog-walking her way to safety.

Meg Mason, author of *Sorrow and Bliss*

There are some things that are too much – the death of someone you love, loss of a relationship or a friend, huge financial hardship or serious illness. Those huge life experiences are different, and we will all manage and sometimes not manage. But in terms of everyday disappointment that you feel keenly but which is, probably, not life changing, I've found the most important thing is to allow myself to feel disappointed, or devastated, or humiliated, or miserable – in other words, own my emotions honestly in the first instance and don't try to pretend I feel all right. But then – and this is key – I try to draw a line under the experience (easier said than done, I know), go for a walk, have a glass of wine or cup of tea, and crucially start the next project. It could be a new book, it could be a new job, but it's better to look forward with hope and possibility rather than brooding on what failed to happen or what you got wrong. In the words of the great Samuel Beckett: 'Try again. Fail again. Fail better.'

Kate Mosse, author of
Warrior Queens and Quiet Revolutionaries

I've had more than my fair share of things going wrong in my life, and the one thing that always grounds me is the birds in my garden. No matter how miserable I am

when I get up in the morning, they will be outside singing to me, waiting for breakfast to magically appear. I
know that I can pull up a chair and look outside my
kitchen window to see sparrows and starlings squabbling over a fat ball before they have a communal bath.
The birds are always there. They rely on me and I rely
on them. No matter what happens or how bad it gets,
seeing a bird on my feeder will always make me smile.

Liz O'Riordan, author of *Under the Knife*

Think about difficult feelings as irritating visitors who
will eventually leave. Like the In-Laws. Work out the
physical symptoms you're experiencing – for example, my
anxiety makes me feel like there's a Dark Overlord Beaver
gnawing on my intestines and a Godzilla stomping on my
inner Tokyo. I find if you characterize them like this and
name them, it makes them easier to deal with.

Maybe you have a pounding in your chest? Could it
be caused by a Gerbil called Ian who has taken up street
dancing (and is pretty bad at it)? Maybe you have a

tight feeling in your tummy? Could that be Barbara and Susan, two Chinchillas who have taken up knitting and are trying to knit your colon into a tea cosy?

Just know that eventually, Ian will need to take a break. And Barbara and Susan will go off to find new knitting patterns. If they don't take the hint, you can try yelling 'SOD OFF BARBARA' or 'SLING YOUR HOOK SUSAN' or 'FUCK OFF IAN AND WHEN YOU GET THERE, FUCK OFF A BIT FUR-THER!' at the top of your voice. This can make you feel better and can also create new and pressing problems that might distract you from what you are feeling.

Georgia Pritchett, author of *My Mess is a Bit of a Life*

In my experience of life, things go wrong a lot. Sometimes these things are small but stressful – my laptop crashes or I forget to renew my passport – but often these things are very big, and very sad, and can feel like things have not just gone wrong but are entirely broken, forever. I felt like this most strongly after my mum died, and then a few years later, more strongly again when my sister died. The existential panic or strung-out claustrophobia or absolutely heartbroken despair – or all of these things at the same time – that arises from these big and small events can leave me with a sense that I am, somehow, undeserving of a place on the planet and that I, unlike everyone else walking around all about me, should just give up on life completely. I know this feeling well. You probably do too. Most of us – all of us, I think – do. And when that feeling takes over me, after a horrible big or small thing happens, I cope and hold steady by working out what it is around me that I can, in fact, control, and which I am, actually, managing quite well.

I find it helpful to visualize the space that I can control around me as very small. That space is smaller than a room, since when things go really wrong, even controlling the room around you can feel impossible. So the space I cling fast to is as small as the volume my two hands make when I cup them together. In that little space I can keep things simple: make a cup of tea that I love (my best tea of all is to make a pot, mixing three bags of something strong like Yorkshire or PG Tips with one bag of something fragrant and beautiful, like lapsang souchong, then to drink the whole pot, with plenty of milk), eat some biscuits or a bit of chocolate I know well, like digestives or a Double Decker, and maybe do something slightly soothing, like light a candle, which can be just a regular tea light as it certainly doesn't have to be something expensive or scented, or find one of the little bottles of lavender oil I keep by my bath and put some of it on my wrists as I drink my tea. All those things are small, comforting, familiar tasks. They ask nothing of me. They have been part of the fabric of my life for decades, and they are all things I can do without having to face the world, spend money, or even attempt to figure anything out.

And doing these tiny, achievable tasks that I can control reminds me that I am brave, and that I have survived many, many things that have gone wrong before, and that I will survive this, too. Because what surviving this stuff has taught me is that the human spirit is a remarkable thing. We survive and endure and eventually, incredibly, thrive through even the worst headache and the most vicious tragedy. And the first steps to surviving, and then thriving, always starts with the little, tiny things you can control, like tea and digestive biscuits.

Clover Stroud, author of *The Red of my Blood*

Pain is inevitable, suffering is optional. As a kidnap negotiator, I got used to things not going according to plan. The key is to learn to stay focused, grounded and calm, no matter what happens. When you perceive things as going wrong, you can surf the waves of emotion as they flood your body. By turning towards whatever it is that has or hasn't happened, rather than away from it – feeling the feeling and dropping the story you associate with causing it – you'll develop a greater awareness. By doing this, you get to work on your very own superpower that enables you to stay calm at the centre of any storm, so you can take personal responsibility for what you do next.

Scott Walker, author of *Order Out of Chaos*

Sometimes I need to remind myself that all I ever wanted to do was write a novel. That's it. Not get it published, not win prizes, not get a mega-ridiculous advance. Just write a novel. And I did that. And that novel didn't even get published. The one I wrote after that became my debut novel. So, actually, everything I have written since that first novel is a bonus. Absolutely everything. Everything I have done is a bonus. So when my career isn't going the way I would like it to, I try to remind myself of that. In terms of my personal life, I really suggest everyone has a WhatsApp group that can act as a safe space to tell people your darkest saddest woes, celebrate the good times, tease out half-thought-through things and make each other laugh. I cannot tell you how much I have benefitted from a WhatsApp group. In fact, I have two that act like that. I don't know what I would do without Chimene and Rosie, or without Musa, Inua, Nish and Vin. Diamonds all of them.

Nikesh Shukla, author of *Your Story Matters*

It always starts with a big cry. I feel ready to rebuild and carry on once I've cried. Afterwards I like to spend time alone. A few peaceful hours listening to an audiobook or podcast while I work on an embroidery project takes me out of my own head for a while. It's become cliché to say having 'me time' is good for mental health, but I really do find slathering on a pricey facemask makes me feel happier, even if it's just because my skin's got a nice glow. Long term, it's having things to look forward to in the diary, booking a table at a nice restaurant, because nothing lifts me more than knowing a good meal awaits.

Chloe Timms, author of *The Seawomen*

This may make you want to rush up and punch me in the face, but if I'm feeling low, I absolutely know I'll feel better by an Act of Kindness. To hopefully mitigate the bile forming at reading such a bloody saintly utterance, this Act of Kindness works just as beautifully if done to yourself.

Kindness, I feel, is one of the most powerful tools of salvation we have – it doesn't cost, and is limitless. But because it's sort of blindingly obvious, it's often overlooked, or, more likely, gently sneered at.

I learned this when I was in the depths of sizeable existential despair, while caring for my dying sister. Actually, I think I learned it after she died. And it's probably gratitude that is the principal ingredient of the kindness that came from that time. Gratitude that I had been able to be there for her, gratitude that she had allowed me, and a completely new and intensely powerful gratitude for life.

Being in a truly, truly horrible place gave me more appreciation, acceptance and compassion for myself and others. Which, without even thinking about it, makes you want to be kind.

Everyone suffers. We all know that. But doing something nice for someone makes you (and fortunately them too) feel better.

Greg Wise, author of *Not That Kind of Love*

'You've been here before Grant and, at the time, it appeared insuperable but you got through it, didn't you?' I tell myself. Then I channel my inner Jake LaMotta, the great prideful pugilist. In a famous 1951 bout, in the midst of being pummelled and bloodied by Sugar Ray Robinson, LaMotta wrapped his arms around the rope of the boxing ring and took every blow from Robinson unanswered, until the referee jumped in and stopped it. At the end of the bout, with the referee raising aloft Robinson's arm to signal he'd won, LaMotta staggered over to his opponent, blood streaming down his battered face and whispered, 'You never got me down, Ray. You never got me down.'

Colin Grant, author of
I'm Black So You Don't Have to Be

I've never been sure if this is advisable or not, but I make lists and I cling to them like life rafts. As long as I can see what has to be done, I can follow the list like a compass and it stops me going under. Obviously this is the very definition of an illusion of control – and as illusions aren't a great foundation for life, I'm not sure how wise this one is. But it works for me.

Decca Aitkenhead, author of *All at Sea*

I go back home to Wolverhampton. Though I'm surprised to find myself admitting it at the age of forty-six. As a kid, my main mission in life was to escape my home town as quickly as possible for London. And the city remains a byword for failure for many in the twenty-first century: not long ago, it was named one of the worst places on earth to live by Lonely Planet, alongside San Salvador and Detroit. If you Google Wolverhampton, one of the news stories that you'll be directed to involves a corpse being discovered in a kebab shop at the end of the street I grew up on.

But it's Wolverhampton's unusual attitude to this ridicule that provides solace: it joins in. When these two stories went viral online, it was people from Wolverhampton who gleefully sent them to me. People from Wales and the north may big up their home towns, but in the West Midlands, we tell war stories. It's part of what makes the people so bloody charming. To put it another way, unlike London, Wolverhampton – one of the least affluent parts of Britain – is totally unpretentious.

There are other cultural differences between the capital and Wolverhampton, from the relative popularity of pies, to the relative tendency for passengers to talk to bus drivers, the relative probability of getting scraps on your fish and chips, the relative acknowledgment between drivers and pedestrians at zebra crossings, the relative amount of clothing worn to go clubbing and the relative chance of getting gravy on your chips. It probably helps that a large chunk of my Punjabi family still live in Wolvo, and to go home is to be among people who will have my back whatever I do. But, let's face it, there is also a larger gap between London and Wolverhampton than there is between London and Paris, and travelling between the two is to truly have a holiday.

Sathnam Sanghera, author of *Empireland*

There are things I've done over the years that have worked to earth me, or settle me: calling my beloved Welsh granny on a Sunday night, and once she died, sitting down on a Sunday night and talking to her anyway; lying on the ground looking up in a beech wood; swimming in the cold river on Dartmoor; listening to the music that resets or wakes me up or heals me; pilgrimages to special places; these are all ways to hold on. Carry on.

But if I'm being honest, the most special thing is the most ordinary. I cook for my family. Every day. It is the miraculous thing that I will never take for granted. On principle, and from experience, I know not to take it for granted.

I cook, I call them down, I scream at them again to come down, I complain, we bicker about normal bollocks, we eat and we talk. Very often I weep during dinner. Tears of quiet joy as they all chat shit about what they got up to, or what we're going to watch, or whatever. My kids laugh at me. They know I'm just overwhelmed by gratitude that I get to love them, feed them, spend time with them, listen to them. I feel rich beyond my wildest dreams, and ready for tomorrow.

Max Porter, author of *Grief is the Thing with Feathers*

Why do we want to write and what stops us? What can we do to overcome the obstacles in our path?

Sunday Times bestselling author Cathy Rentzenbrink shows you how to tackle all this and more in *Write It All Down,* a guide to putting your life on the page. Complete with a compendium of advice from amazing writers such as Dolly Alderton, Maggie O'Farrell and Lemn Sissay, this beautiful book will help you discover the pleasure and solace to be found in writing a memoir.

Out now.